W9-AYN-610

Kindle Fire™ HD

FOR

DUMMIES®

POCKET EDITION

Kindle Fire™ HD
FOR
DUMMIES®
POCKET EDITION

by Nancy C. Muir and Harvey Chute

John Wiley & Sons, Inc.

Kindle Fire™ HD For Dummies,®Pocket Edition

Published by
John Wiley & Sons, Inc.
111 River Street
Hoboken, NJ 07030-5774

www.wiley.com

For general information on our other products and services, please contact our Customer Care Department within the U.S. at 877-762-2974, outside the U.S. at 317-572-3993, or fax 317-572-4002. For technical support, please visit www.wiley.com/techsupport.

Wiley publishes in a variety of print and electronic formats and by print-on-demand. ISBN 978-1-118-53075-7 (paper); ISBN 978-1-118-54712-0 (e-pub); ISBN 978-1-118-54714-4 (e-mobi); ISBN 978-1-118-54720-5 (e-PDF)

Manufactured in the United States of America

10 9 8 7 6 5 4 3 2 1

WILEY

About the Authors

Harvey Chute maintains KindleBoards.com, a blog and message board community dedicated to all things Kindle. He was also co-author on *Kindle Touch For Dummies.* An IT program manager in his day job, Harvey enjoys gadgets, technology, and books from a wide variety of genres. He and his wife and daughters all share a love of reading, and enjoy their houseful of Kindle e-readers.

Nancy Muir is the author of over 100 technology books on topics ranging from tablet computers and popular computer applications to nanotechnology. Her website TechSmart Senior (www.techsmartsenior.com) provides information for those reading her bestselling books *Computers For Seniors For Dummies* and *Laptops For Seniors For Dummies* (both published by Wiley) and for those discovering technology later in their lives. She contributes a column on computers and the Internet at www.retirenet.com. Prior to her writing career, Nancy was a manager in both the publishing and computer software industries.

Publisher's Acknowledgments

We're proud of this book; please send us your comments at http://dummies.custhelp.com. For other comments, please contact our Customer Care Department within the U.S. at 877-762-2974, outside the U.S. at 317-572-3993, or fax 317-572-4002.

Some of the people who helped bring this book to market include the following:

Acquisitions and Editorial

Project Editor: Annie Sullivan

Sr. Acquisitions Editor: Katie Mohr

Copy Editor: Annie Sullivan

Technical Editor: Earl Boysen

Cover Photo: © RonTech2000/ iStockphoto.com (background); image of device by Harvey Chute

Composition Services

Project Coordinator: Kristie Rees

Layout and Graphics: Christin Swinford

Proofreader: Joni Heredia Language Services

Publishing and Editorial for Technology Dummies

Richard Swadley, Vice President and Executive Group Publisher

Andy Cummings, Vice President and Publisher

Mary Bednarek, Executive Acquisitions Director

Mary C. Corder, Editorial Director

Publishing for Consumer Dummies

Kathleen Nebenhaus, Vice President and Executive Publisher

Composition Services

Debbie Stailey, Director of Composition Services

Table of Contents

· ·

Introduction

● ●

Kindle Fire HD is a very affordable way to access all kinds of media, from music and videos to books and colorful magazines. It's also a device that allows you to browse the Internet, check your e-mail, and read documents. Its portability makes it incredibly useful for people on the go in today's fast-paced world.

In this book, I introduce you to all the cool features of Kindle Fire HD, providing tips and advice for getting the most out of this ingenious little tablet. I help you find your way around its attractive and easy-to-use interface, and I even recommend some neat apps that make your device more functional and fun.

"If Kindle Fire HD is so easy to use, why do I need a book?" you may be asking yourself. When I first sat down with Kindle Fire HD, it took about three or four days of poking around to find settings, features, and ways to buy and locate my content and apps. When was the last time you had four days to spare? I've spent the time so that you can quickly and easily get the hang of all the Kindle Fire HD features and discover a few tricks I bet your friends won't uncover for quite a while.

Icons Used in This Book

Icons are little pictures in the margin of this book that alert you to special types of advice or information, including

These short words of advice draw your attention to faster, easier, or alternative ways of getting things done with Kindle Fire HD.

 When you see this icon, you'll know that I'm emphasizing important information for you to keep in mind as you work with a particular feature.

 There aren't too many ways you can get in trouble with the Kindle Fire HD, but in those few situations where some action might be irreversible, I include warnings so you avoid any pitfalls.

Get Going!

Time to get that Kindle Fire HD out of its box, set it up, and get going with all the entertaining options it makes available to you. Have fun!

Chapter 1

Overview of the Kindle Fire HD

. . . .

In This Chapter

▶ Comparing Kindle Fire HD to the competition

▶ Surveying all the features of the Kindle Fire HD

. . . .

*A*mazon, the giant online retailer, just happens to have access to more content (music, movies, audio books, and so on) than just about anybody on the planet. And now, the Kindle Fire HD, an awesome machine in its own right, offers the key to that treasure chest of content.

In this chapter, you get an overview of the Kindle Fire HD: how it compares to competing devices and its key features.

How Kindle Fire HD Stacks Up

Let's start at the beginning. A *tablet* is a handheld computer with an onscreen keyboard and apps that allow you to play games, read e-books, check e-mail, browse the web, and more.

In the world of tablets, the first device to hit big was iPad, and then subsequent tablets, such as Samsung Galaxy, HP TouchPad, and the original Kindle Fire tablet, appeared. The iPad has the largest foothold in the market up to now, so the logical comparison here is to the iPad, specifically to the newest iPad model – sometimes referred to as iPad 3.

First, look at the Kindle Fire models currently available. You can choose from two display sizes: a 7-inch display and an 8.9-inch display. Here are the configuration options available for each Kindle Fire model:

- ✔ **Kindle Fire HD with 7-inch display.** Available with 16GB or 32GB of memory.

- ✔ **Kindle Fire HD with 8.9-inch display.** Available with 16GB or 32GB of memory.

- ✔ **Kindle Fire HD, 8.9-inch display, with 4G LTE.** Available with 32GB or 64GB of memory.

- ✔ **Kindle Fire (non-HD) with 7-inch display.** Available with 8GB of memory.

With these options in mind, take a look at how Kindle Fire HD compares to iPad.

All models of Kindle Fire HD are lighter and smaller than iPad. The 7-inch Kindle Fire HD (see Figure 1-1) weighs only 13.9 ounces, and the 8.9-inch Kindle Fire HD weighs only 20 ounces. This compares to iPad's 9.7-inch display and 1.44-pound frame. That smaller and lighter form factor makes the Kindle Fire HD easier to hold with one hand than the iPad.

The Kindle Fire HD 7-inch model has a projected battery life of eleven hours, versus iPad's ten hours. The high-definition screen resolution on the Kindle Fire HD's bright color screen is about on par with the iPad screen; both tablets display pixels at a resolution that is finer than human eyes can detect.

Figure 1-1: The neat size and weight of Kindle Fire HD make it easy to hold.

Kindle Fire HD models have internal storage options from 16GB up to 64GB for the Kindle Fire HD 4G LTE. This is comparable to the 16, 32, or 64GB options for the various iPad models. Beyond that, Amazon provides free storage for all your Amazon-purchased content in the *Cloud* (a huge collection of online storage) so you can stream video and music instead of downloading it, if you like.

Kindle Fire HD also has some very intelligent technology that allows your browser to take advantage of the Cloud to display your web pages faster.

Kindle Fire HD has a front-facing camera, which is currently limited to use with Skype for video calls. It has a built-in microphone and dual stereo speakers. iPad has a microphone, a single speaker, and, unlike the Kindle Fire HD, both front-facing and back-facing cameras. iPad also has a built-in GPS, whereas Kindle Fire HD models use Wi-Fi for location services.

In several ways, Kindle Fire HD is easy to use with a simple Android-based touchscreen interface, and it's a great device for consuming media — and what a lot of media Amazon makes available! Kindle Fire HD also offers Amazon's Silk browser, an e-mail client, and the fabulous Kindle e-reader (see Figure 1-2).

Key Features of Kindle Fire HD

Kindle Fire HD is one spiffy little device with all the things most people want from a tablet packed into an easy-to-hold package: e-mail, web browsing, players for video and music content, an e-reader, a great online content store, access to tens of thousands of Android apps, and so on. In the following sections, you get to explore all these great features.

Pre-installed functionality

Here's a rundown of the functionality you get out of the box from pre-installed apps:

- ✔ E-reader to read both books and periodicals
- ✔ Music player
- ✔ Video player
- ✔ Apps for Contacts, Calendar, OfficeSuite, and Skype
- ✔ Document reader for Word, PDF, RTF, and HTML format files

- ✔ Silk web browser
- ✔ Photo viewing
- ✔ E-mail client (meaning you can set up Kindle Fire HD to access your existing e-mail accounts)

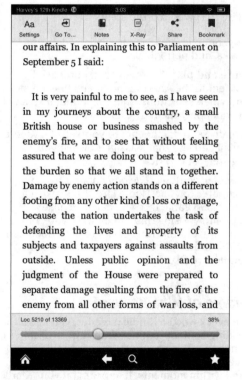

Figure 1-2: Where it all started, with Kindle e-reader functionality.

The free version of OfficeSuite comes pre-installed on your Kindle Fire HD. This app offers a mini-suite of productivity products, including a document viewer for Microsoft Word files, a spreadsheet viewer for Excel documents, and a presentation viewer for PowerPoint briefings.

Kindle Fire HD gives you the ability to

- ✔ **Buy.** Shop at Amazon for music, video, apps, books, and periodicals.
- ✔ **Store and play.** Store Amazon-purchased content in the Amazon Cloud and play music and video selections from the Cloud, instead of downloading them to your device.
- ✔ **E-mail.** Send documents to yourself at a Kindle e-mail address that's assigned when you register your device.
- ✔ **Transfer content.** *Sideload* content from your computer to your Kindle Fire HD by using a Micro USB cable that you can purchase separately. Using this cable (see Figure 1-3), you can copy photos, music, videos, and documents (Word or PDF) from any source onto your Kindle Fire HD.

The magic of Whispersync

If you've ever owned a Kindle e-reader, you know that downloading content to it has always been seamless. All you need for this process is access to Wi-Fi or to the 3G cellular network. Then, you simply order a book, and within moments, it appears on your Kindle device.

Kindle Fire HD enjoys the same kind of easy download capability for books, music, video, and periodicals.

Figure 1-3: The Micro USB cable, sold separately for around $10.

Whispersync helps sync items such as bookmarks you've placed in e-books or the last place you watched in a video across various devices. For example, say you have the Kindle e-reader app on your Kindle Fire HD, PC, and smartphone. Wherever you left off reading, whatever notes you entered, and whatever pages you've bookmarked will be synced among all the devices without you having to lift a finger.

Content, content, content!

Kindle Fire HD is meant as a device you use to consume media, meaning that you can play/read all kinds of music, movies, TV shows, podcasts, e-books, magazines, and newspapers. Amazon has built up a huge amount of content, from e-books (1.2 million titles and counting in the Kindle Store) to audiobooks (100,000 titles), movies and TV shows (120,000 movies and TV series), music (20 million songs), and hundreds of your favorite magazines.

You can find various kinds of content in the Amazon store by clicking the Store button in the libraries you access through the Kindle Fire HD Home screen. Tap Books or Audiobooks to browse the huge selection available. Tap Newsstand to shop for periodicals (see Figure 1-4) and Music to shop for songs and albums. Tap Videos to go directly to the Amazon VideoStore. Tap Apps to shop the Amazon Appstore, and tap Games to browse gaming titles in the Appstore. All the content you purchase is backed up on the Amazon Cloud.

See Chapter 4 for more about buying content and apps for your Kindle Fire HD.

 You can also transfer documents from your computer or send them via e-mail and read them on Kindle Fire HD. Note that documents are not backed up in the Amazon Cloud.

Browsing with Amazon Silk

Silk is Amazon's web browser (see Figure 1-5). Silk is simple to use, but the real benefits of Amazon Silk are all about browsing performance.

Amazon Silk is touted as a "Cloud-accelerated split browser." In plain English, this means that the browser can use the power of Amazon's servers to load the pages of a website quickly. Because parts of the process of loading web pages are handled not on Kindle Fire HD, but on servers in the Cloud, your pages simply display faster.

Figure 1-4: Amazon's magazine selection is constantly growing.

In addition, you get what's called a *persistent connection*, which means that your tablet is always connected to the Amazon Internet backbone (the routes that data travels to move among networks online) whenever it has access to a Wi-Fi connection.

Figure 1-5: Amazon Silk offers simple-to-use browsing tools.

Another fascinating ability of Silk is the way it filters content to deliver it faster. Say you open a news site, such as MSN or CNN. Obviously, millions of others are accessing these pages on the same day. If most of those folks choose to open the Entertainment page after reading the home page of the site, Silk essentially predicts what page you might open next and pre-loads it. If you choose to go to that page, too, it appears instantly.

Taking advantage of free Cloud storage

Kindle Fire HD models have considerable storage space (up to 64GB). In addition to that, when you own a Kindle Fire HD, you get free, unlimited Cloud storage for all digital content purchased from Amazon (not the content you copy onto Kindle Fire HD from your computer by using a Micro USB cable). This means that books, movies, music, and apps are held online for you to stream or download at any time, instead of being stored on your Kindle Fire HD.

This storage means that you don't use up your Kindle Fire HD memory. As long as you have a Wi-Fi connection (or a 4G LTE connection), you can stream content from Amazon's Cloud at anytime. If you'll be away from a connection, download an item (such as an episode of your favorite TV show) and watch it, and then remove it from your device when you're done. The content is still available in the Cloud: You can download that content again or stream it anytime you like.

A world of color on the durable display

The display on Kindle Fire HD offers a high-definition display and 16 million colors (see Figure 1-6). *In-plane switching (IPS)* is a technology that gives you a wide viewing angle on the Kindle Fire HD screen. Amazon has taken IPS one step further by adhering a polarizing filter to the display, enabling vivid color and contrast to be displayed from any viewing angle. The result is that if you want to share your movie with a friend sitting next to you on the couch, she'll have no problem seeing what's on the screen from that side angle.

Figure 1-6: The bright display on Kindle Fire HD makes media shine.

In addition, the glass screen is coated with layers that make it extra strong — 30 times harder than plastic — so it should withstand most of the bumps and scratches you throw at it.

Of course, you should avoid dropping your Kindle Fire HD, exposing it to extreme temperatures, or spilling liquids on it. The User Guide also advises that, if you do spill liquids, you shouldn't heat the device in your microwave to dry it.

Understanding the value of Amazon Prime

Kindle Fire HD comes with one free month of Amazon Prime. During your free month, Prime will allow you to get a lot of perks, such as free two-day shipping on thousands of items sold through Amazon and free instant videos.

If you decide to pick up the service after your free month, it will cost you $79 a year. So, what do you get for your money?

Prime includes free two-day shipping on millions of items and overnight shipping for only $3.99. Not every item offered on Amazon is eligible for Prime, but enough are that it's a wonderful savings in time and money over the course of a year. You can probably pay for the membership with the free shipping on the first two or three orders you place.

In addition, Prime membership gives you access to Prime Instant Videos, which includes thousands of movies and TV shows that can be streamed to your Kindle Fire HD absolutely free.

 If you already have a paid Amazon Prime account, you don't get an extra month for free, sad to say. And if you don't have a Prime account, your 30 days of a free account starts from the time you activate your Kindle Fire HD, not the first time you make a Prime purchase or stream a Prime Instant Video.

Chapter 2

Kindle Fire HD Quickstart

• •

In This Chapter

▶ Setting up your Kindle Fire HD

▶ Playing with libraries, the Carousel, and Favorites

▶ Using a Micro USB cable to transfer data

• •

*I*n this chapter, I help you to get familiar with what comes in the box, explore the interface (what you see on the screen), and start to use your fingers to interact with the touchscreen.

Get Going with Kindle Fire HD

The first time you turn on Kindle Fire HD, you register it and link it to your Amazon account so that you can shop till you drop. Although your device probably comes with a decent battery charge, at some point you'll have to charge the battery. I cover that in the section "Charging the battery," later in this chapter.

Opening the box

Your Kindle Fire HD arrives in an elegant black box (see Figure 2-1). The Kindle Fire HD itself rests on top of a piece of hard plastic, and a small black card with some Kindle Fire HD basics printed on both sides is slotted into the lid of the box. Beneath the piece of plastic rests a charger in a paper sleeve. That's it.

Remove the protective plastic from the device, and you're ready to get going.

Figure 2-1: The Kindle Fire HD packaging.

Turning the device on and off

After you get the tablet out of its packaging, it's time to turn it on. The Kindle Fire HD sports a Power button on the top of the device when you hold it in portrait orientation (see Figure 2-2). Next to the Power button are volume control buttons and a headphone jack.

Figure 2-2: The Power button sits on the top edge of your Kindle Fire HD.

To turn the device on, press the Power button. If you're starting up for the first time, you're taken through a series of setup screens (see the following section for more about this). After you go through the setup process and register your Kindle Fire HD, you see the Home screen shown in Figure 2-3 on startup. The Status bar gives you information about items such as your device's battery charge, the current time, wireless signal strength, and any notifications about recent downloads or apps installed.

If you want to lock your Kindle Fire HD, which is akin to putting a laptop computer to sleep, tap the Power button again. To shut down your Kindle, press and hold the Power button briefly until a message appears offering you the options to Shut Down or Cancel.

 If your Kindle Fire HD becomes non-responsive, you can press and hold the Power button for 20 seconds, and it should come to life again.

Figure 2-3: The Kindle Fire HD Home screen.

Getting to know the touchscreen

Before you work through the setup screens for your
Kindle Fire HD, it will help if you to get to know the
basics of navigating the touchscreen — especially if
you've never used a touchscreen before:

> ✔ **Tapping.** Tap an item to select it or double-tap
> an item (such as an app) to open it.

✔ **Locking.** If your Kindle Fire HD goes to a lock screen after a period of inactivity, swipe your finger from right to left from the padlock icon (see Figure 2-4) to go to the Home screen.

✔ **Double-tapping.** Double-tap to enlarge text and double-tap again to return the text to its original size. Note, this works only in certain locations, such as when displaying a web page in the Silk browser.

Figure 2-4: Swipe to the left from the padlock icon to go to the Home screen.

✔ **Zooming.** Place your fingers apart on a screen and pinch them together to zoom in on the current view; place your fingers together on the screen and then move them apart (unpinch) to enlarge the view.

✔ **Swiping left to right.** Swipe left to move to the next page in apps such as the e-reader or the Silk web browser. Swipe to the right to move to the previous page.

✔ **Swiping up and down.** Swipe up and down to scroll up and down a web page.

These touchscreen gestures will help you get around most of the content and setup screens you encounter.

Setting up your Kindle Fire HD

When you turn Kindle Fire HD on for the first time, you see a series of screens that help you set up and register the device. Don't worry: There aren't many questions, and you know all the answers.

The first screen is titled Welcome to Kindle Fire. This is the point in the setup process at which you connect to a Wi-Fi network. You need this connection to register your device.

At some point during this setup procedure you may be prompted to plug your adapter in if your battery charge is low. You may also be notified that the latest Kindle software is downloading and have to wait for that process to complete before you can move forward.

Follow these steps to register and set up your Kindle Fire HD:

1. **In the Connect to a Network list, tap an available network.**

Kindle Fire HD connects to the network (you may
need to enter a password and then tap Connect
to access an available network) and then displays
the Register Your Kindle screen (see Figure 2-5).

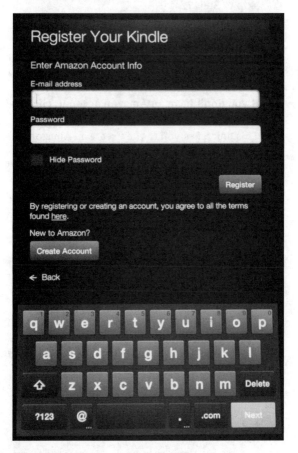

Figure 2-5: Register your Kindle Fire HD to use it.

2. **On the Register Your Kindle screen that appears (see Figure 2-5), enter your Amazon account information (e-mail address and a password), tap the Register button, and then skip to Step 7.**

   See Step 3 if you don't have an Amazon account.

   You can choose to select the Hide Password checkbox so that your password doesn't appear on your screen as you type it. This protects your password from prying eyes.

3. **If you don't have an Amazon account, click the Create Account link.**

   This link takes you to the Create an Amazon Account screen, with fields for entering your name, e-mail address, and password (which you have to retype to confirm).

4. **Enter this information, and then tap Continue.**

5. **If you want to read the terms of registration, tap the By Registering, You Agree to All of the Terms Found Here link.**

6. **When you finish reading the terms, tap the Close button to return to the registration screen.**

7. **To complete the registration, tap the Register button. At this point the Select Your Time Zone screen is displayed.**

8. **Tap to select a time zone from the list provided, as shown in Figure 2-6.**

   For countries other than the United States, tap Select another Time Zone and choose from the provided list. Then, tap the Back button in the bottom-left corner to return to the Time Zone screen.

9. **Tap Continue.**

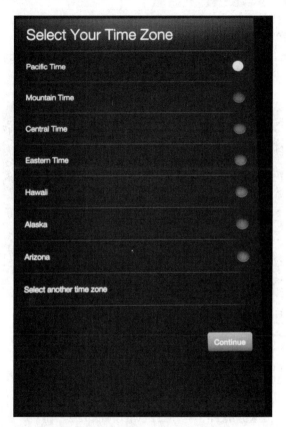

Figure 2-6: Choose your time zone.

A final screen appears saying Confirm Account.
There's also a link labeled Not *<Your Name>*? If, for
some reason, you aren't you (for example, you may
have entered your account information incorrectly),
tap the Not *<Your Name>* link to change your account
information. Otherwise, tap the Continue link.

The next screen displayed is the Get Started screen, which allows you to link your Kindle Fire HD with your Facebook and Twitter accounts, as shown in Figure 2-7. Doing so makes it easy to share recommendations with your friends and followers.

Figure 2-7: Link accounts with the Get Started screen.

This is the point at which the Kindle Fire HD may download the latest Kindle software. Sit back, relax, and anticipate using your new toy.

You can view a series of quick tips to get you started with Kindle Fire HD, as shown in Figure 2-8. (If you need more help at any time, you can refer to the User's Guide in the Kindle Fire HD Docs library.) Tap Next to move through this tour; on the last of the nine screens, tap Close to get going with Kindle Fire HD.

Charging the battery

Kindle Fire HD has a battery life of eleven hours for Wi-Fi–connected activities, such as web browsing, streaming movies, and listening to music from the Cloud. If you're a bookworm who's more into the printed word than media, you can get even more battery life with wireless turned off.

Figure 2-8: This very quick tutorial covers the basics of using Kindle Fire HD.

You charge the battery with the provided charger. Attach the smaller end of the charger to your Kindle Fire HD's Micro USB port, located on the right side of the device, and the other end to a USB port – in a PC/Mac, or on a USB wall charger. If completely depleted, the Kindle Fire HD takes about four hours to charge with a wall charger, or about 13.5 hours with a computer USB connection.

 There's a battery indicator on the Status bar that runs across the top of the Kindle Fire HD screen so you can check to see if your battery is running low.

Getting to Know the Interface

The interface you see on the Kindle Home screen (see Figure 2-9) is made up of three areas. At the top, you see a set of buttons that take you to the Kindle Fire HD libraries that contain various types of content. In the middle of the screen is the Carousel. The Carousel contains images of items you recently used that you can flick with your finger to scroll through and tap to open. Finally, the bottom portion of the Home screen shows items related to the center item in your carousel. For example, it will show Customers Also Bought items related to the book, app, or music track in your carousel.

Accessing Kindle Fire HD libraries

Kindle Fire HD libraries are where you access downloaded content, as well as content stored by Amazon in the Cloud. Libraries (with the exception of the Docs library) also offer a Store button that you can tap to go online to browse and buy more content.

Figure 2-9: This graphical interface is fun to move around with the flick of a finger.

Tap any library button to open a library of downloaded and archived content: Games, Apps, Books, Music, Videos, Newsstand, or Audiobooks.

Note a few additional buttons: a Shop button to buy digital or physical items from Amazon; a Web button to browse the Internet; a Photos button to view your photo gallery; a Docs button, where documents that you sideload from your computer or receive as e-mail attachments in your Kindle inbox are placed; and an Offers button to view special advertisements from Amazon.

The Video app opens to the Amazon store, rather than a library, because in most cases, it's not very prudent to download video content to your Kindle Fire HD. Because this type of content takes up so much of your memory, it's preferable to play video from Amazon's Cloud (which is called *streaming*).

 There's also a Web button at the far right that you can tap to open the Silk web browser. Find out more about going online and using the browser in Chapter 5.

In a library, such as the Music library shown in Figure 2-10, you can tap the Device or Cloud tab. The Device tab shows you only content you have down-loaded; the Cloud tab displays all your purchases or free content stored in Amazon's Cloud library, including content you've downloaded to the Kindle Fire HD.

You can download archived content at any time or remove downloaded content to the Cloud. You can also view the contents of libraries in different ways, depending on which library you're in. For example, you can view Music library contents by categories such as Songs, Artists, Playlists, and Albums.

 When you go to a library and tap the Cloud button, content that is currently downloaded sports a small checkmark. If no checkmark is present, you can download the content by tapping the item at any time and then tapping Download.

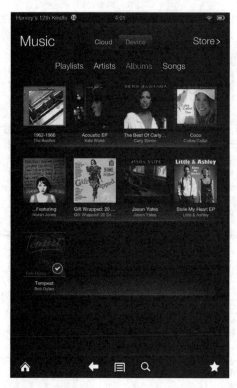

Figure 2-10: Your Music library provides access to all your musical content.

It's possible to download video, which is useful if you'll be out of range of a wireless connection. But I recommend removing the content from your device when you're done watching. Removing content from Kindle Fire HD involves pressing it with your finger and choosing Remove from Device from the menu that appears.

Understanding the Cloud

Everything you buy using Kindle Fire HD is purchased through Amazon or its affiliates on the Amazon site. That content is downloaded to your device through a technology called *Whispersync*, which requires a wireless connection.

When you purchase content, you can choose whether to keep it in the Cloud or download it to your Kindle Fire HD. If you download it, you can access it whether or not you're in range of a wireless network. At any time, you can remove content from the device, and it is archived in the Cloud for you to stream to your device (music or video) or re-download (music, video, books, and magazines) whenever you like.

As mentioned before, you can also sideload content you've obtained from other sources, such as iTunes, to your Kindle Fire HD libraries. Sideloading involves using the Micro USB cable that came with your device, and then using the cable to connect Kindle Fire HD to your computer and copying content to Kindle Fire HD. See the section "Using a Micro USB Cable to Transfer Data," later in this chapter, for more about this process.

Playing with the Carousel

If you've used an Android device, such as a smartphone, you've probably encountered the Carousel concept. On Kindle Fire HD, items you've used recently are displayed chronologically in the Carousel (see Figure 2-11), with the most recent item you used on top. You can swipe your finger to the right or left to flick through the Carousel contents. When you find an item you want to view or play, tap to open it.

Whatever you tap opens in the associated player or reader. Music will open in the Amazon MP3 music player; video in the Amazon Video player; and docs, books, and magazines in the Kindle e-reader.

Figure 2-11: Kindle Fire HD's Carousel makes recently used content readily available.

 When you first begin using Kindle Fire HD, before you've accessed any content, by default the Carousel contains the Amazon Kindle User Guide. It may also contain recently used content from your Amazon Cloud library or that you've accessed from other registered Kindle devices that you may have.

 To remove an item from the Carousel, press and hold your finger on it; then tap Remove from Carousel from the menu that appears.

Organizing Favorites

When you're on a roll using Kindle Fire HD for accessing all kinds of content, the Carousel can get a bit crowded.

You may have to swipe five or six times to find what you need. That's where Favorites comes in.

If, for example, you open a particular book often or play a certain piece of music frequently, place it in the Favorites area of the Kindle Fire HD Home screen so you can find it more quickly.

By default, Favorites includes the Amazon Silk web browser, e-mail, help, and the IMDb movie database app. To pin an item to Favorites, press and hold it in the Carousel or a library, and then select Add to Favorites from the menu that appears (see Figure 2-12).

To remove content from Favorites, press and hold the item and choose Remove from Favorites or Delete from the menu that appears. Remove from Favorites unpins the item from Favorites, although it's still available to you on the Carousel and in the related library. Delete removes the item from the device (although it's still archived in Amazon's Cloud).

To view favorites at any time, press the star-shaped button in the lower right corner of the Home page.

Getting clues from the Status bar

The Status bar runs across the top of every Kindle Fire HD screen, just like the Status bar on your mobile phone. This bar, shown in Figure 2-13, provides information about your battery charge, current time, and wireless connectivity. By swiping down on the Status bar, you can access your Kindle Fire HD settings.

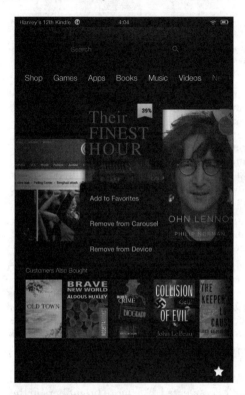

Figure 2-12: Pin items to Favorites by using this menu.

Figure 2-13: Tools and settings available on the Status bar.

Here's a rundown of what you'll find on the Status bar:

✔ **Device name:** First is the name of your Kindle Fire HD, such as Harvey's Kindle or Harvey's 12th Kindle.

✔ **Notifications:** A number in a circle next to the name of your device indicates the number of pending Notifications. Notifications can come from the Kindle Fire HD system announcing a completed download or the e-mail client announcing that a new e-mail has arrived, for example. To view all your notifications, swipe down on the Status bar and a list appears (see Figure 2-14).

✔ **Current time:** The next item on the Status bar is the current time, based on the time zone you specified when setting up the Kindle Fire HD.

✔ **Quick Settings:** Swipe down on the Status bar to access Quick Settings. Quick Settings offers the most commonly used settings. Use these items to adjust volume, brightness, or your Wi-Fi connection, for example. To access the full Kindle Fire HD Settings menu, tap More (see Figure 2-15).

✔ **Wi-Fi Connection:** The item on the Status bar to the right of Quick Settings is an icon showing you the Wi-Fi connection status. If this is lit up, you're connected. The more bright bars in the symbol, the stronger the connection.

✔ **Battery charge:** Finally, there's an icon that indicates the charge remaining on your battery.

The Options bar

The Options bar runs along the bottom of your Kindle Fire HD screen. The items offered on the Options bar change, depending on what library or app you're using, but they always include a Home button. Also often available are items, such as Search, to run a search in features such as a content library. In addition, you'll almost always see a Menu button when you tap the Options bar. This icon makes available commonly used actions, such as those for accessing settings for the currently displayed feature. Figure 2-16 shows you the options available on the Music library screen.

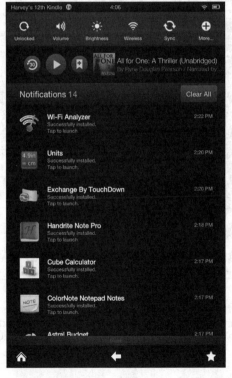

Figure 2-14: The list of current notifications that you can display from any screen.

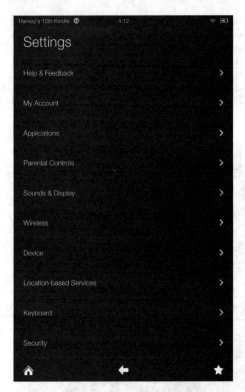

Figure 2-15: Use the Quick Settings menu and tap More to access the full complement of settings for Kindle Fire HD.

Use the Home button to jump back to the Kindle Fire HD from anywhere. On some screens where it would be annoying to be distracted by the Options bar, such as the e-reader, you may have to tap the bottom of the screen to make the Options bar appear.

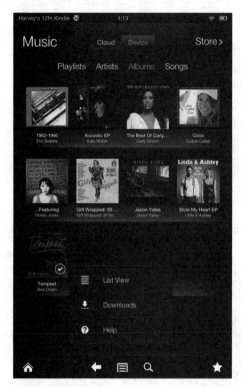

Figure 2-16: The Options bar offers contextually relevant options, depending on which screen is displayed.

Using a Micro USB Cable to Transfer Data

It's easy to purchase or rent content from Amazon, which you can choose to download directly to your Kindle Fire HD or stream from Amazon Cloud.

However, you may want to get content from other places, such as iTunes or your Pictures folder on your computer, and play or view it on your Kindle Fire HD.

To transfer content to Kindle Fire HD, use the Micro USB cable that came with your device. This cable has a USB connector on one end that you can plug into your PC or Mac and a Micro USB connector on the other that fits into the slot on your Kindle Fire HD (which is located on the right side of the device).

Note the two port connectors on the right side of your Kindle Fire HD: an HDMI-out port and a Micro USB port. They look similar and are un-labeled. The Micro USB port is nearer the top of the device.

Attach the Micro USB end to your Kindle Fire HD and the USB end to your computer. Your Kindle Fire HD should then appear as a drive in Windows Explorer or the Mac Finder. You can now click and drag files from your hard drive to the Kindle Fire HD or use the copy and paste functions to accomplish the same thing.

Using this process, you can transfer apps, photos, docs, music, e-books, and videos from your computer to your Kindle Fire HD. Then, just tap the relevant library (such as Books for e-books and Music for songs) to read or play the content on your Kindle Fire HD.

 You can also upload content to your Amazon Cloud library on your computer, and that content will then be available on your Kindle Fire HD from the Cloud. See Chapter 6 for more about how this process works.

Chapter 3

Kindle Fire HD Settings

• •

In This Chapter

▶ Opening your Kindle Fire's settings

▶ Working with Quick Settings

▶ Delving into the Kindle Fire settings

• •

*W*hen you first take your Kindle Fire HD out of the box, Amazon has provided you with default settings. However, you can personalize the settings to make Kindle Fire HD work uniquely for you.

Some of these settings are discussed in the chapters that cover individual apps, such as the Amazon video player (Chapter 6). I cover the more general settings in this chapter.

Opening Quick Settings

In this fast-paced day and age, quick is the name of the game for most of us. Amazon has provided you with Quick Settings to streamline your settings experience.

You access both a short list of commonly used settings and all the more detailed settings for Kindle Fire HD by swiping down in the Status bar area at the top of the screen.

Here are the settings that you can control from the Quick Settings menu (see Figure 3-1):

Figure 3-1: Quick Settings control the settings that you access most often.

- ✔ **Unlocked/Lock:** This is a toggle feature, meaning that you tap it to lock your device into portrait or landscape mode.

- ✔ **Volume:** Tap Volume to display a slider bar that you can use to increase or decrease the volume (see Figure 3-2).

- ✔ **Brightness:** You can use the slider beneath this setting (see Figure 3-3) to adjust the brightness manually. You can also tap the Automatic Brightness On/Off buttons to turn on or off a feature that controls the brightness of the screen based on ambient light.

- ✔ **Wireless:** Tap to display the Airplane Mode On/Off button (see Figure 3-4) that you can use to turn wireless on or off. When you turn Wi-Fi on, a list of available networks appears. Tap an available network to join it. Note that you may be asked to enter a password to access some networks.

- ✔ **Sync:** Generally speaking, if you're within range of a Wi-Fi network, when you begin to download content, it downloads very quickly. However, if you've been out of range of a network, you might want to use this setting when you're back in range of a network to manually initiate the download of new content or continue downloads that may have been interrupted.

Figure 3-2: Controls that appear when you tap Volume.

Figure 3-3: Adjust brightness manually by using this slider.

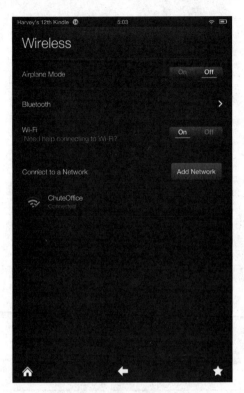

Figure 3-4: Choose from the list of available networks.

Finding Other Settings

Beyond what I discuss in the preceding section, there is one more item on the Quick Settings menu — More. Figure 3-5 shows you the many settings that appear when you tap the More button.

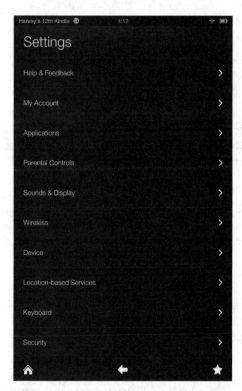

Figure 3-5: Plenty more settings are revealed when you tap More.

These settings include: Help and Feedback, My Account, Applications, Parental Controls, Sounds & Display, Wireless, Device, Location-based Services, Keyboard, Security, and Legal & Compliance.

You won't need to change many of these settings very often because the way Kindle Fire HD works out of the box is usually very intuitive. But if you do find that you want to make an adjustment to settings, it's useful to know what's available.

The following sections give you the skinny on what settings appear when you tap More in the Quick Settings menu.

Help & Feedback

When you tap Help & Feedback from Settings, you see the screen shown in Figure 3-6, which offers a world of help and allows you to interact with Amazon customer service.

The Help & Feedback screen includes four somewhat self-explanatory sections: Getting Started, User Guide, Customer Service, and Feedback. The last two tabs display a form in which you can type a message to send on to Amazon. Here's how these four options work:

- ✔ **Getting Started:** Use this tab, shown in Figure 3-7, to get help with the following topics: Your Kindle, at a Glance; Connecting Wirelessly, Set Up Your Kindle; and Kindle Support Pages.

- ✔ **User Guide:** This option brings up the table of contents for the Kindle Fire HD user guide. You can click a link to drill down on any of nineteen topic areas.

- ✔ **Customer Service:** The first question you have to answer here is "What can we help you with?" Use the Select an Issue drop-down list to locate a related issue and tap the Back button. You can also tap the Select Issue Details drop-down list, choose a more specific topic, and then tap the Back button. Choose from the How Would You Like to Contact Us field by selecting either E-mail or Phone.

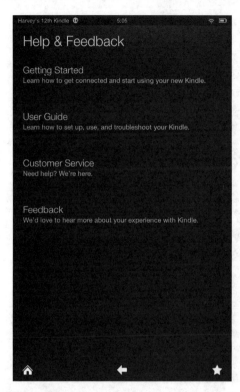

Figure 3-6: Help & Feedback settings for Kindle Fire HD.

✔ **Feedback:** Tap Select a Feature and choose
from the list that appears (items such as
Newsstand, Books, Docs, and so on). Then,
enter your comment in the Tell Us What You
Think about This Feature field. You can also tap
one to five stars to rate the feature you're providing feedback on (see Figure 3-8). Tap the
Send Feedback button to submit your thoughts
to Amazon.

Figure 3-7: The Getting Started page leads you to help on a variety of topics.

My Account

Kindle Fire HD does much of what it does by accessing your Amazon account. You need to have an Amazon account to shop, access the Amazon Cloud library online, and register your Kindle Fire HD.

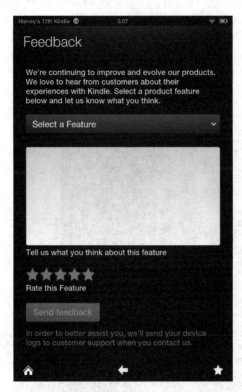

Figure 3-8: The Feedback tab of Help & Feedback gives you a forum for your opinions.

The My Account option in Settings provides information about the account to which the device is registered (see Figure 3-9). To remove this account from your Kindle Fire, you can tap the Deregister button. Because the obvious thing to do next is to register your Kindle Fire to another account (because so much depends on your having an associated account), you then are presented with a Register

button. Tap Register and fill in your Amazon user-
name and password to register the device.

From this screen you can also manage your social
network accounts (currently Facebook and Twitter),
and your e-mail accounts.

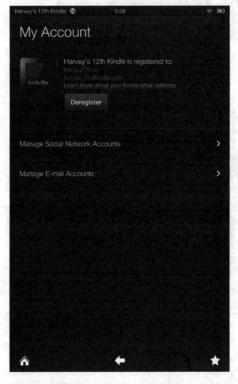

Figure 3-9: Check which Amazon account your device is
registered to.

Applications

Apps can help you do everything from manage e-mail to play games. Managing the way apps work on your Kindle Fire HD is done through the Applications settings.

When you tap Applications in Settings, you see several options followed by a list of Amazon Applications (see Figure 3-10).

The Notifications Settings option lets you control which applications can alert you with Notifications. Most of these default to "on," but some have to be explicitly turned on, such as e-mail notifications. Use the On/Off button beside each application to turn notifications on and off.

The next option is Installed Applications. Tap that to see all of the apps installed on your device.

Tap any of these apps, and you encounter the following options:

- ✓ **Force Stop:** Force Stop allows Kindle Fire to stop an application from running if it encounters problems.

- ✓ **Uninstall:** This option only appears for 3rd party apps; Amazon apps that are needed for your Kindle Fire HD to operate cannot be uninstalled. Uninstall removes the app from your Kindle Fire HD. Keep in mind, though, that although the app is uninstalled, if you purchased it from Amazon, it's still archived in the Cloud.

- ✓ **Storage:** You can clear Kindle Fire HD's memory of data stored by the app by tapping the Clear Data button.

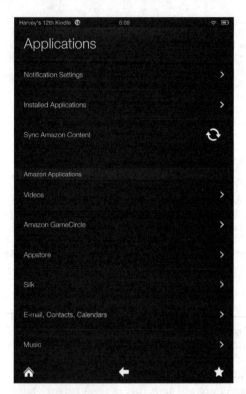

Figure 3-10: Each application on your Kindle Fire HD has associated settings.

> ✔ **Cache:** Computing devices store data based on
>   your usage to more quickly provide the data
>   you need. This so-called cache of data fills up a
>   bit of memory, so if you want to free up some
>   memory, tap the Clear Cache button.
>
> ✔ **Launch by Default:** Tap this button to launch an
>   app automatically when you turn on Kindle Fire.

✔ **Permissions:** A list of permissions to allow
access to information that this app might have
to use to perform its function, such as your
location.

Below the Installed Applications option, a Sync
Amazon Content button is displayed. You can press
that to have your Kindle Fire HD updated with any
pending downloads.

Following that is a list of Amazon Applications. You
can tap any of those to view and adjust any application-
specific settings.

Parental Controls

Kindle Fire HD now has a way to let you manage and
restrict purchasing, content types, web browsing, and
other parental controls.

Tap the Parental Controls option under the Settings
menu to view the simple on/off buttons, as shown in
Figure 3-11.

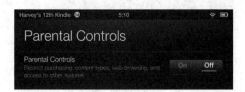

Figure 3-11: Turn Parental Controls on by tapping the On
button.

Tap the On button to turn on Parental Controls. You'll
be asked for a password of at least 4 characters. At
this point you'll see the set of Parental Control
options as shown in Figure 3-12.

Turn off or block various features of your Kindle Fire
HD by tapping the appropriate setting from this
screen.

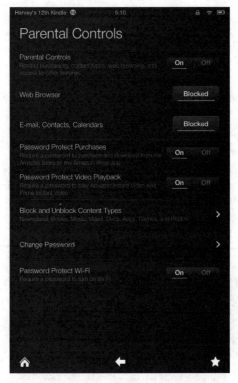

Figure 3-12: Turn off or block various features from the
Parental Controls screen.

Sounds and Display

With a tablet that's so media-centric, it's important that you know how to control the volume and adjust the display. If you tap Sounds & Display in Kindle Settings, you see various items (see Figure 3-13): a volume slider and various sound and display settings.

You can use the volume slider to move the volume up or down, as an alternative to the physical buttons at the top edge of your Kindle Fire HD.

You can also turn off Dolby Digital Plus, although there is little reason to do so as it enhances sound quality.

The next two settings control Notifications alerts. Notifications may come from the arrival of a new e-mail, a completed download, or an app notification (such as an appointment reminder from a calendar app that you may have downloaded). You can mute all notifications by checking that option, or modify Notification Sounds by selecting from the list of sound options available.

Following that are three screen-related options. Turn on Auto Brightness to have the Kindle Fire HD's lighting automatically dim or increase in intensity, depending on the ambient light conditions.

If the Auto Brightness option is turned off, you can manually adjust the brightness of the display using the slider that appears on this screen.

Finally, you can adjust the length of time you want to elapse before your screen goes to sleep using the Screen Timeout setting.

Figure 3-13: Sound and Display settings are pretty simple to use.

Wireless

Wireless is a pretty essential setting for using Kindle Fire HD. Without a wireless connection, you can't stream video or music, shop at the various Amazon stores, or send and receive e-mail. Wireless can refer to Wi-Fi, or in the case of the Kindle Fire HD 4G LTE, it can refer to the wireless cellular data network.

A new feature for Kindle Fire HD is the addition of Bluetooth capability, which lets you connect your Kindle Fire HD wirelessly to Bluetooth devices.

Tap Wireless to view these settings (see Figure 3-14):

✔ **Airplane Mode:** This option turns Wireless off and displays an airplane symbol in the status bar.

✔ **Bluetooth:** This allows you to turn Bluetooth on or off and to select a Bluetooth device that's near you.

✔ **Wi-Fi:** Turn Wi-Fi on or off. With Wi-Fi on, you can click an item in the list of available networks, and Kindle Fire HD connects to that network.

✔ **Connect to a Network:** Tap this setting to enter a new network's SSID (the public name of a Wi-Fi network) and security information to add it to the list of available networks. You should only need this if the Wi-Fi network you want to attach to does not broadcast its network name.

Device

You can check your Kindle Fire HD device settings (see Figure 3-15) to find out facts such as the remaining storage space available or your device's serial number. This is also where you can reset your Kindle Fire HD its factory settings.

Here are the device settings available to you:

✔ **About:** Relates to the operating system version for your Kindle Fire HD.

✔ **Storage:** Tells you how much memory is still available on your device.

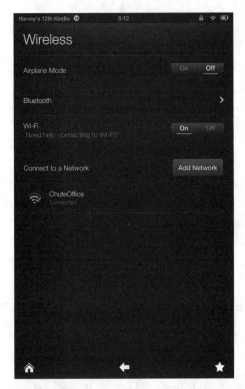

Figure 3-14: Turn on and choose your preferred Wi-Fi network.

- ✔ **Battery:** Indicates the percentage of battery power remaining.
- ✔ **Date & Time:** Allows you to change the time zone and the time format (24-hour versus am/pm format).

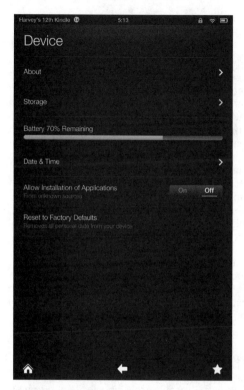

Figure 3-15: Device settings provide a lot of information about the status of your device.

✔ **Allow Installation of Applications:** Kindle Fire HD is set up to get its content from Amazon because that provides some measure of security. For example, apps you sideload from your computer to Kindle Fire HD that are from third-party suppliers are more likely to introduce viruses to your computer. Still, you can buy apps elsewhere and port them over from your

computer. If you want to allow this, choose On
in this setting. If you don't want to let apps
other than those verified by Amazon to be
placed on your Kindle Fire HD, tap Off.

✔ **Reset to Factory Defaults:** If you sold your
Kindle Fire HD to somebody, you wouldn't want
that person to have your docs and contact information. Also, if you've loaded a lot of content on
your Kindle Fire HD and then decide you want a
clean beginning to clear up memory, you might
choose to reset the device. Resetting wipes all
content and any changes you've made to default
settings. If you tap this setting, you see the confirming dialog box shown in Figure 3-16. Tap
Erase Everything to continue with the reset procedure or Cancel to close the warning dialog
box and halt the reset.

Although you get considerable storage with
Kindle Fire HD, a chunk of that is taken up with
pre-installed and system files. So the storage
available may indicate that you have only a portion of the total storage available on the device.

Location-based Services

Your Kindle Fire HD can use location data for apps
and websites that provide location services, such as
map applications and geotagging. This is off by
default; with this settings screen, you can turn it On
or Off, as shown in Figure 3-17. When you turn it on, a
confirmation screen appears; click OK to approve the
use of location services.

Note: the Kindle Fire HD does not have an internal
GPS, but it uses wireless signals to approximate the
location of the device.

Figure 3-16: This dialog box appears asking if you want to revert to factory defaults.

Keyboard

There's no physical keyboard with your Kindle Fire HD, so you depend on its onscreen keyboard to provide input to apps such as Quickoffice or in fields used to search and enter text into forms, such as e-mail messages.

Figure 3-17: Enable or disable location-based services with this setting.

There are five simple things you can do with Kindle Fire HD Keyboard settings (see Figure 3-18):

> ✔ **Auto-Capitalization:** This function automatically capitalizes the first word in a sentence. This feature defaults to "On," but you can turn it off if you wish with this setting.

Figure 3-18: Control your onscreen keyboard with these settings.

✔ **Sound on Keypress:** If you like that satisfying clicky sound when you tap a key on the onscreen keyboard, tap to turn this setting on.

✔ **Auto Correction:** Your Kindle Fire HD will automatically correct misspellings when the space bar is pressed or punctuation is used. With this setting, you can turn this off or tune it to modest, aggressive, or very aggressive levels.

- ✔ **Show Correction Suggestions:** When typing, your Kindle Fire HD can offer suggestions for corrected text. You can have this Always Show, Show on Portrait Mode, or Always Hide.

- ✔ **Spelling Suggestions:** This setting lets you turn On or Off the highlighting of misspelled words in text fields.

Security

The first thing you can do to keep your Kindle Fire HD secure is to never let it out of your hands. But because we can't control everything and sometimes things get lost or stolen, it's a good idea to assign a password that's required to unlock your Kindle Fire screen. If a thief or other person gets his hands on your Kindle Fire, there's no way he can get at stored data, such as your Amazon account information or contacts.

Tap the Security Settings option, and you'll see these simple choices (see Figure 3-19):

- ✔ **Lock Screen Password:** Simply tap On, and fields appear labeled New PIN and Confirm PIN. (You can select a simple numeric PIN or an alphanumeric password.) Tap in the New PIN field and, using the onscreen keyboard that appears, type a password. Tap in the Confirm PIN field and retype the password. Tap Finish to save your new password.

- ✔ **Credential Storage:** Credentials are typically used for Microsoft Exchange–based accounts, such as an account you use to access e-mail on your company's server. If you use Microsoft Exchange, it's a good idea to get your network administrator's help to make these settings.

✔ **VPN:** This option provides you a link to the Amazon Appstore, where you can download an app to enable you to connect to a Virtual Private Network.

✔ **Device Administrators:** If your device is being administered through a company Exchange account, use this setting to establish the device administrator who can modify settings for the account.

✔ **Enable ADB:** This security option enables Kindle app developers to debug applications over a USB connection.

 You have to get an app if you want to set up Kindle Fire HD to work with Microsoft Exchange accounts. Try Exchange by Touchdown, which you can get from the Amazon Appstore by tapping Apps on your Home screen.

Legal & Compliance

This settings option simply displays legal notices, terms of use, product safety and compliance information, and Amazon's privacy policy.

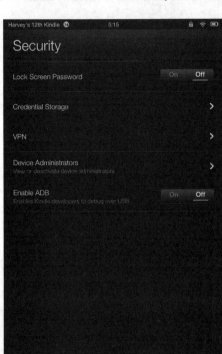

Figure 3-19: The Security settings offer five settings related to securing your Kindle Fire.

Chapter 4

Going Shopping

. . . .

In This Chapter

▶ Using your Amazon account

▶ Shopping at the Amazon Appstore

▶ Buying apps, music, video, and print

▶ Buying other Amazon items through your Kindle Fire HD

. . . .

*A*mazon offers both a rich supply of books, magazines, music, and video, and an Amazon Appstore that you can use to get your hands on apps that add to the functionality of your Kindle Fire HD. These apps can range from simple utilities such as a calculator to fun and addictive games and even a word processor or spreadsheet.

In this chapter, you discover how to get apps, as well as books and other content for your Kindle Fire HD.

Managing Your Amazon Account

You buy things from Amazon by using the account and payment information you provide when you create an Amazon account. You probably have an account if you ever bought anything on Amazon (or opened an account when you bought your Kindle Fire HD). To buy things on Amazon with your Kindle Fire HD, you need to have associated your Amazon account with your Kindle Fire HD, which happens during the setup process covered in Chapter 2.

After you associate your device with an Amazon account, you manage account settings by going to the Amazon website by using the browser on either your Kindle Fire HD or computer and then tapping or clicking (depending on whether you're using a touchscreen device) Your Account in the top-right corner of the Amazon screen. You can then tap/click Manage Payment Options or Add a Credit or Debit Card from the Payment section of your account, and then change or enter a new method of payment and billing address.

Visiting the Amazon Appstore

After you create an Amazon account (which I discuss in the preceding section), you can shop for all kinds of content from your Kindle Fire HD. I'll start by introducing you to the world of apps.

Apps provide you with functionality of all kinds, from an app that turns your Kindle Fire HD into a star-gazing instrument to game apps. You can find calendar apps, drawing apps, and apps that provide maps so that you can find your way in the world.

Exploring the world of apps

You can buy apps for your Kindle Fire HD by using the Amazon Appstore. This store is full of apps written especially for devices that are based on the Android platform, including Kindle Fire HD.

 Android devices may have slightly different operating systems, and therefore, not every app will work on every device. See Chapter 7 for some suggested apps that will work well with your Kindle Fire HD.

Follow these steps to explore the world of apps:

1. **Tap the Apps button at the top of the Home screen to enter your Apps library.**

2. **Tap the Store button.**

   The store shown in Figure 4-1 appears.

Figure 4-1: The Amazon Appstore.

At the top of the store are links to various categories of apps. Below that is the offer *Today's Free App of the Day*.

3. **(Optional) Tap this option to download a free app to your device.**

The links at the top of the display are:

- ✔ **Best Sellers:** This link displays the current list of top-selling apps.

- ✔ **Games:** Tap this link to see featured game titles, as shown in Figure 4-2. Across the top of the Games section of the store are links such as Action, Arcade, Casual, Puzzles, and All Games.

- ✔ **New Releases:** This link displays the latest apps that have been added to the store.

- ✔ **All Categories:** Tap this link to see all categories of games.

The All Categories link takes you to a long list of app categories, including Books & Comics, City Info, Cooking, Education, Entertainment, Finance, Health & Fitness, Music, Photography, Reference, Utilities, and many more.

From the main Apps page you can see the Free App of the Day, Highly Rated Apps, and Recommended For You. The Recommended For You area shows personalized recommendations in that category based on your buying history.

Searching for apps

You can have fun browsing through categories of apps, but if you know which app you want to buy, using the search feature can take you right to it.

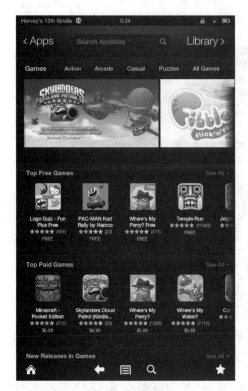

Figure 4-2: Games includes puzzles, cards, sports, and more.

To search for an app, follow these steps:

1. **Tap in the Search Appstore field.**

   The keyboard shown in Figure 4-3 appears.

2. **Using the onscreen keyboard, enter the name of an app, such as the game Angry Birds Rio.**

   Suggestions appear beneath the Search field.

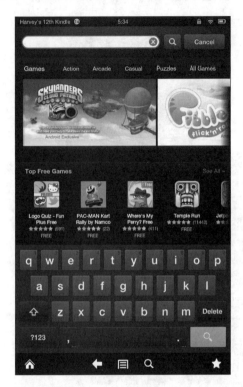

Figure 4-3: Use the search field and onscreen keyboard in the Appstore to find what you want.

3. **Tap a suggestion to display the list of suggestions with more detailed results.**

4. **Tap an app name to see more details about it.**

   The Product Info screen appears, as shown in Figure 4-4. You're shown screenshots from the app, along with a description, recommendations, customer reviews, product details and developer information.

Figure 4-4: Product details are shown in the Product Info screen.

The Save For Later button adds the app to your Saved for Later list. You access this list by tapping the Menu button on the Options bar at the bottom of the display, and then tapping Saved for Later. You can go to this list at any time to buy an item. You can delete it from the list by pressing the Saved button on the app's Product Info page. At that point, the button will be replaced with the original Save For Later button.

Buying apps

You might find something you want to own by browsing or searching, but however you find it, when you're ready to buy, you can follow these steps:

1. **From the product description, tap the orange button that displays the price.**

   Note that if the app is free, this button reads Free, but if you have to pay for the app, the app price (such as $0.99) is displayed on the button. When you tap the button, its label changes to Get App.

2. **Tap the button again to purchase paid apps and download paid or free apps to your Kindle Fire HD.**

   A Downloading button appears, showing the download progress. When the installation is complete, an Open button appears.

3. **If you want to use the app immediately, tap the Open button.**

To use the app at any time, locate it in the App library or, if you've used it recently, on the Carousel; tap the app to open it. Each app has its own controls and settings, so look for a settings menu like the one for the Angry Birds Rio game, shown in Figure 4-5.

You can also buy apps from the Appstore on your PC or Mac. When placing the app in your shopping cart, be sure to select Kindle Fire HD for the device you want to download the app to in the drop-down list below the Add to Cart button. When you complete your purchase, the app is immediately downloaded to your Kindle Fire HD.

To delete an installed app from your App library, press and hold it until a menu appears. Tap Remove from Device. The app isn't gone. It's still stored in the Cloud, and you can download it again at any time by tapping it in the Cloud tab of the App library.

Figure 4-5: App settings for Angry Birds Rio.

Buying Content

From Amazon, you can buy publications, books, music, and video (movies and TV shows) to download or stream to your Kindle Fire HD. The buying process is somewhat similar for the different types of content, but there are slight variations, which I explain in the following sections.

Buying publications

Kindle Fire HD's color display makes browsing through color magazines especially appealing. If you tap Newsstand on the Home page of Kindle Fire HD, and then tap the Store button, you see several categories of items (see Figure 4-6).

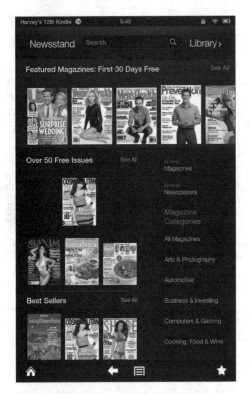

Figure 4-6: The Newsstand Store.

Featured Magazines are displayed across the top. You can swipe right to left to scroll horizontally.

Below Featured Magazines, you see magazine covers for free issues and best sellers. In the column on the right you see browse options for Magazines and Newspapers, followed by categories. Categories include Arts & Photography, Automotive, Computers & Gaming, Cooking, Food & Wine, Family & Parenting, and many more. Tap the All Magazines button to see a complete list of available magazines.

When you find the publication you want, follow these steps to buy or subscribe to it:

1. **Tap the item.**

   A screen appears showing pricing, a description of the publication, and Subscribe Now and Buy Issue buttons.

2. **Tap Subscribe Now or Buy Issue.**

   The button changes to a box showing the Downloading status. When the download is complete, the button label changes to Read Now.

3. **Tap the Read Now button to open the magazine.**

   Note that the magazine is stored in your Amazon Cloud library, where you can read or download it to your Kindle Fire HD at a later time.

Buying books

If you've joined the electronic book revolution (or even if you haven't), you'll find that reading books on Kindle Fire HD is convenient and economical (e-books are typically a few dollars less than the print version, and you can borrow e-books from your local library for free).

To browse through e-books from Amazon on your Kindle Fire HD, follow these steps:

1. **Tap the Books button on the Kindle Fire HD Home screen.**

2. **Tap the Store button.**

   The Amazon Bookstore sports a Recommended for You section at the top, recommending books based on your buying history.

3. **Swipe right to left to scroll horizontally through the recommendations at the top.**

    You also see categories such as Kindle Select 25, Best Sellers, Monthly Deals under $4, Children's Picture Books, Editors' Picks, and New & Noteworthy.

As with the Newsstand, when you locate and tap an item in the bookstore, you see a screen with that item's pricing and description (see Figure 4-7). In the bookstore, the buttons you see at this point are labeled Buy for (price), Try a Sample, and Add to Wish List. Here's how these three buttons work:

- **Buy for (price):** Tap this button, and the button changes to a Downloading meter and then to a Read Now button. Tap the Read Now button to open the book. Remember that the book is now stored in your Books library, where you can tap it to open and read it at your leisure.

- **Try A Sample:** Tap this button, and it changes to a Processing message and then to a Read Now button. Tap the Read Now button to open the sample of the book.

- **Add to Wish List:** Tap this button, and a small form appears where you can select a Wish List. Press OK, and the book will be added to your Amazon Wish List where you can find it later to sample or buy.

After you've read a bit of your new book, it will appear both in your Books library and on the Carousel on the Home screen.

To remove a book from your device (remembering that it will still be stored in the Amazon Cloud), open your Book library, press and hold the book, and tap Remove from Device from the menu that appears.

Figure 4-7: Details about a book in the Amazon Bookstore.

Buying music

No matter what kind of music you prefer, from hip-hop to Broadway, you're likely to find a great many selections tucked away in Amazon's vaults.

Tap the Music button on the Kindle Fire HD Home screen, and then tap the Store button. On the Store screen, various features will be displayed, such as New Releases, any special promotions, and Recommended For You. On the right side of the screen, you see the following links: Bestsellers, New Releases, and Genres. Tap one of these links to get a list of items in that category (see Figure 4-8). You can also tap the Albums or Songs buttons to view music by these criteria.

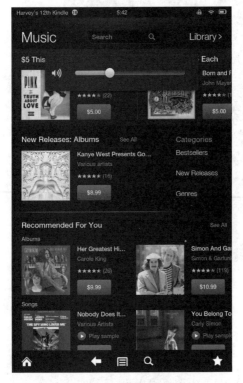

Figure 4-8: The Amazon Music Store.

From anywhere in the Music Store, you'll see thumb-nails of music selections. Follow these steps to buy music:

1. **Tap an item.**

   A screen appears, displaying a list of the songs, in the case of an album, with Price buttons for both the entire album and each individual song.

2. **Tap the arrow button to the left of a song to play a preview of it.**

3. **Tap a Price button.**

   The button label changes from the price of the item to the word Buy.

4. **Tap the Buy button.**

   The song or album downloads to your Music library. A confirmation dialog box opens, display-ing a Go to Your Library button and a Continue Shopping button (see Figure 4-9).

5. **Tap the Go to Your Library button to open the album and display the list of songs.**

   The album is now stored both in your Music library and the Cloud. If you tap on a song to play it, it'll also appear with recently accessed content in the Carousel.

 If you tap the Continue Shopping button, you can later find the album in your Music library.

See Chapter 6 for more about playing music.

Buying video

You should definitely check out the experience of consuming your video programs on a portable device such as Kindle Fire HD. From lying in bed or on the beach to watching your videos while waiting in line at the bank, portability can be a very convenient feature.

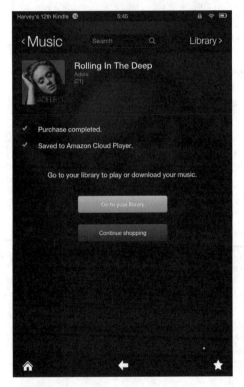

Figure 4-9: This dialog box allows you to return to your library or keep shopping.

When you tap Video on the Kindle Fire HD Home screen, you're instantly taken to the Amazon Video Store shown in Figure 4-10.

Figure 4-10: Shop for video in the Amazon Video Store.

Along with any special promotions, you see thumbnails of items in various categories, including Prime Instant Video, Next Up, Movies, TV Shows, and For the Kids. Each of these categories has a horizontally scrolling list of thumbnails for videos.

Tap an item, and a descriptive screen appears. For TV shows, this screen includes episode prices and a set of Season tabs. For movies, this screen offers a Watch

Trailer button and purchase/rental options such as Rent, Rent HD, Buy, and Buy HD (see Figure 4-11). The purchase/rental options available can vary for different movies.

Tap an episode Price button or a movie Rent or buy button, and the button becomes a green confirmation button. Tap that button, and it becomes a Watch Now button. Tap the Watch Now button, and the TV show or movie starts to play.

Tap the 48 Hour Rental button for movies, and you see a Rent button. Tap this, and you're immediately charged for the rental. The 48-hour rental period begins when you start to watch the movie.

See Chapter 6 for more about playing videos.

Shopping for Anything Else

Amazon kindly pre-installed an Amazon Shopping app on your Kindle Fire HD so that you can quickly go to their online store and buy anything your heart desires.

Tap the Shop link from the Home page. A screen opens with a dynamically-changing featured item. Below that are shopping links for Digital items as well as physical products.

Now, just proceed to shop as you usually do on Amazon.

Figure 4-11: The video screen offers several options.

Chapter 5

Getting Online

• •

In This Chapter

▶ Using Wireless on your Kindle Fire HD

▶ Browsing the web with Silk

▶ Personalizing Silk's settings

▶ Setting up e-mail

• •

Kindle Fire HD can become your new go-to device for keeping informed and in touch by using Amazon's Silk browser and the pre-installed e-mail client.

In this chapter, you discover the ins and outs of browsing with Silk and the simple tools you can use to send and receive e-mail on Kindle Fire HD.

Getting Online by Using Wi-Fi

All Kindle Fire HD models have Wi-Fi features, meaning that if you have access to a nearby Wi-Fi network, you can use that to go online. You might access a Wi-Fi connection through your home network, at work, or via a public hotspot, such as an Internet café or airport.

(In addition, the Kindle Fire HD 4G LTE has wireless access through the cellular data network. This requires a prepaid service plan for the cellular data access. In this section, we'll focus on the Wi-Fi access that all Kindle Fire HD models support.)

When you first set up your Kindle Fire HD (as described in Chapter 2), you can choose a Wi-Fi network to use for going online. If you want to log on to a different network, follow these steps:

1. **Swipe down from the top of the screen to open a menu of common settings, such as Volume, Brightness, and Wireless.**

2. **Tap Wireless.**

   Your Wireless settings appear (see Figure 5-1).

3. **Tap a network in the list of available wireless networks to sign in.**

   You have to enter a password to sign in to some networks.

Browsing with Silk

Silk is a browser that takes advantage of Amazon's ability to use its own servers to make your browsing experience fast.

For example, if you visit a popular news website and choose to tap the headline story to get more details, the odds are many thousands of people have done the same thing. The Silk browser recognizes this pattern and holds that next page in its cache (a dedicated block of memory) to deliver it quickly to you if you also make this selection. This ability makes your browsing experience fast and smooth as, well, silk.

In the following sections, I introduce you to Silk's browser environment. Many tools and features will be familiar to you from other browsers, but a few are unique to Silk.

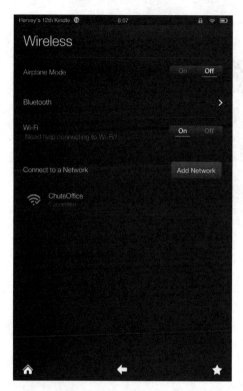

Figure 5-1: Use Wi-Fi settings to select a network to join.

Using navigation tools

From the Kindle Fire HD Home screen, scroll to the right in the list of links at the top by swiping left until you see the Web link. Tap on the Web link to see Silk, as shown in Figure 5-2.

Bookmarks   Address/Search   Add tab
button   field   button

Back   Forward Menu
button   button button

Figure 5-2: Silk offers a familiar browser interface.

You can tap the Back Arrow and Forward Arrow icons to move among pages you've previously viewed. To go directly to a page, tap in the Address field (note

that this field will act as a Search field if you enter a
word or phrase or as an Address field if you enter a
website's address, or URL). Enter a site address, and
tap Go. The website is displayed.

Silk uses tabs that allow you to display more than one
web page at a time and move among those pages. Tap
the Add Tab button — which features a plus sign (+) —
to add a tab in the browser. When you do, thumbnails
of recently visited sites appear. You can tap on a
thumbnail to go to that site, or you can tap in the
Address bar and enter a URL by using the onscreen
keyboard that appears.

Bookmarking sites

You can bookmark sites in Silk so that you can easily
jump back to those sites again. With a site displayed
on screen, tap the Add Bookmark button to the left of
the Address bar. In the Add Bookmark dialog box that
appears (see Figure 5-3), tap OK to bookmark the currently displayed page.

To see your bookmarks, tap the Menu button, and
then tap the Starter Page option. A page appears with
links for Starter, Bookmarks, and History. You can
then tap the Bookmarks link to display thumbnails of
all bookmarked pages. Tap on one to go there.

To delete a bookmark, view the web page in the
Silk browser, and simply tap the Add Bookmark
button again to the left of the Address bar. A
pop-up message will appear confirming that the
bookmark has been removed.

When a website is open in Silk, the Menu button
on the Options bar also provides a Share Page feature. When you tap this option, you can select to
share the current page via Facebook or via Skype.

Searching for content on a page

Web pages can contain a lot of content, so it's not always easy to find the article or discussion you want to view on a particular topic. Most browsers provide a feature to search for content on a web page, and Silk is no exception.

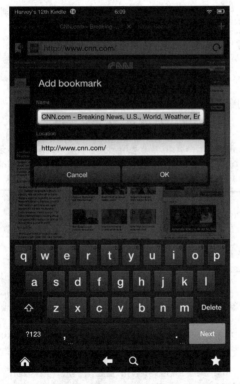

Figure 5-3: Setting bookmarks helps you return to a favorite web page.

To search the currently displayed page by using Silk, follow these steps:

1. **Tap Menu on the Options bar.**

2. **On the screen that appears (see Figure 5-4), tap Find in Page.**

   The onscreen keyboard appears with the Search field active.

3. **Type a search term.**

Figure 5-4: Search the currently displayed page.

It appears in an orange box hovering above the first instance of the word on the page. Other instances of the word on that page are highlighted in yellow, as shown in Figure 5-5.

4. **Tap the Up or Down arrows beside the search field to jump to the next instance of the word on that page.**

5. Tap Done to end the search.

Figure 5-5: The first instance of a word on a page is indicated by an orange box.

Searching the web

Search engines make our lives easier because they help us narrow down what we're looking for by using specific search terms; they then troll the web to find matches for those terms from a variety of sources.

To search the entire web, follow these steps:

1. **Tap the plus sign (+) to add a tab in the browser if you want search results to appear on a new tab.**

   Thumbnails of recently visited sites appear.

2. **Tap in the Search field.**

   The thumbnails change to a list of bookmarked or recently visited sites, and the onscreen keyboard appears.

3. **Enter a Search term and tap Go.**

   By default, search results appear in Bing.

4. Tap a result to go to that page.

 To specify a search engine to use other than the default, Bing, tap the Menu button in the Options bar, and then tap Settings. Use the Search Engine option to choose Google, Bing, or Yahoo! as the default search engine.

Reviewing browsing history

We've all experienced this: You know you visited a site in the last day or so that had a great deal, product, news story, or whatever — but you just can't remember the URL of the site. That's where the ability to review your browsing history comes in handy. Using this feature, you can scan the sites you visited recently organized by day and, more often than not, spot the place you want to revisit.

With Silk open and displaying a web page, tap the
Menu button on the Options bar. Tap Starter Page
and then History, and sites you've visited on the
Kindle Fire HD appear in a list divided into categories
such as Today, Yesterday, and Last 7 Days. Look over
these sites, and, when you find the one you want, tap
it to go there.

Working with web page content

Using your Kindle Fire HD, you can do several things
with the contents of websites. For example, you may
find online content that you want to download, such
as a PDF file that you download to your Docs library
or an image you download to the photo Gallery. You
can also open or share content you find online.

Here's how these work:

- ✔ **View downloads.** Tap Menu on the Options bar,
  and then tap the Downloads button to view
  completed downloads.

- ✔ **Save or view images.** Press and hold an image,
  and a menu appears offering various options,
  including the option to Save Image or View
  Image (see Figure 5-6).

- ✔ **Open, save, or share links.** Press and hold your
  finger on any linked text until a menu appears
  offering these options: Open, Open in New Tab,
  Open in Background Tab, Bookmark Link, Share
  Link, and Copy Link URL.

Personalizing Silk

Silk sports a nice, clean interface. Still, you can
personalize the way Silk looks and acts so that it
might work better for you.

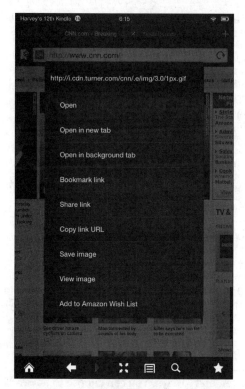

Figure 5-6: You can work with links and images on your Kindle Fire HD by using this menu.

With Silk open, tap the Menu button on the Options bar, and then tap Settings. The screen that appears lists some of the things you can control about the Silk interface:

✔ **Requested Website view:** Lets you specify mobile or desktop versions of websites or have the browser decide automatically.

✔ **Load Images:** Allows images on web pages to be displayed in the browser.

You can double-tap a page to enlarge the view and double-tap again to reduce the view. Or with your fingers pinched together on the screen, spread them out to enlarge the view. Start with your fingers spread apart, and then pinch them together to reduce the view size.

You can get rid of all the personalized settings you've made to Silk. With Silk open, on the Options bar, tap the Menu button and then Settings. Then, tap Reset All settings to Default.

Making Privacy Settings

The Privacy settings for Silk help you to stay safe when you're browsing online. Tap the Menu button on the Options bar, and then tap Settings to view and modify the following privacy settings (see Figure 5-7). You may have to scroll up or down to see all of the privacy-related settings options.

✔ **Block pop-up windows.** Tapping this setting opens a dialog box that offers the settings Ask, Never, and Always. You can choose to have Silk ask you whether it should open pop-up windows, never allow pop-ups at all, or always allow pop-ups by tapping the relevant setting.

✔ **Accelerate page loading.** This option, which is On by default, tells your browser to use Amazon's servers to speed up your browsing experience. If you don't want to go through Amazon's servers, you can turn off this option by tapping the check-marked box. Some people find that browsing speed increases for them when this option is turned off.

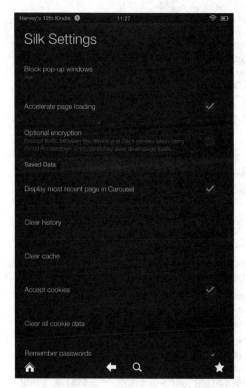

Figure 5-7: Privacy settings can protect your personal information as you browse.

✔ **Optional encryption.** This option is available only when Accelerate page loading is turned On. Turning it on encrypts, or disguises, any information sent from your device to Amazon's servers. Note that turning it on may slow down your web browser performance.

✔ **Display most recent page in Carousel.** By default, your Carousel shows the most recent item you've viewed, including web pages. You can exclude web pages from appearing in the Carousel by tapping the check-marked box to remove the check-mark.

✔ **Clear history.** Your Silk browser retains a history of your browsing activity to make it easy for you to revisit a site. However, it's possible for others who view your browsing history to draw conclusions about your online habits. To clear your history, tap OK in this setting.

✔ **Clear cache.** Any computing device holds information in its cache to help it redisplay a page you've visited recently, for example. To clear out that cache, which can also free up some memory on your Kindle Fire HD, tap OK.

✔ **Accept cookies.** Tap this checkbox to stop sites from downloading cookies to your Kindle Fire HD.

✔ **Clear all cookie data.** You can tap this setting, and then in the Clear dialog box that appears, tap OK to clear all cookies from your device.

✔ **Remember passwords.** If you want Silk to remember passwords that you enter for various accounts, tap this checkbox. Just be aware that this setting puts your accounts at risk should you ever misplace your Kindle Fire HD. One option, if you use this setting, is to require a password to unlock your Kindle Fire HD Home screen. This setting, which can help protect all content stored on the device, is discussed in Chapter 3.

If you scroll up or down, you'll see other settings, including:

✔ **Clear Form Data.** This clears out any form data you've already saved.

✔ **Enable Location.** This allows sites to request access to your current location.

✔ **Clear Location Access.** This clears out any location access that websites may have gathered.

Working with E-Mail

Kindle Fire HD has a built-in e-mail client that allows you to access e-mail accounts you've set up through various providers, such as Gmail and Windows Live Hotmail. You can then open the inboxes of these accounts and read, reply to, and forward messages by using your Kindle Fire HD. You can also create and send new messages, and even include attachments.

In the following sections, I provide information about setting up and using your e-mail accounts on Kindle Fire HD.

Setting up an e-mail account

Setting up your e-mail on Kindle Fire HD involves providing information about one or more e-mail accounts that you've already established with a provider such as Gmail.

Follow these steps to set up an e-mail account the first time you use the app:

1. **Tap Apps.**

   The Apps library appears.

2. **Tap E-mail.**

   The e-mail app opens and displays a list of account types.

3. **Tap AOL, Exchange, Gmail, Hotmail, Yahoo, or Other Provider.**

The dialog box shown in Figure 5-8 appears.

4. **Enter your name, e-mail address, password, and description in the appropriate fields, and then tap Next.**

   A new screen appears that lets you set synchronization options for contacts or calendar. Press the Save button.

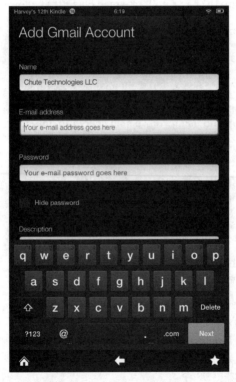

Figure 5-8: The screen for setting up your e-mail account.

5. **A Setup Complete screen displays with options to View Inbox, Go to Account Settings, or Add Another Account.**

You can set up as many e-mail accounts as you like. When you open the Kindle Fire HD Email app, you see a Unified Inbox that combines messages from all accounts you set up, as well as individual inboxes for each account (see Figure 5-9).

Figure 5-9: Your Kindle Fire HD e-mail client inboxes.

To delete an account in the Email app, tap the Menu button in the Options bar and then tap Settings. Tap an account; from the screen that appears, tap Remove Account near the bottom of the screen.

Sending e-mail

After you set up your e-mail account(s), as described in the preceding section, you're able to send e-mails from your Kindle Fire HD. To create and send an e-mail, with the Email app open, follow these steps:

1. **Tap the Inbox icon, and then tap the New button.**

   The New button is in the top right corner of the screen.

   A blank e-mail form appears.

2. **In the To: field, enter a name.**

   Alternatively, tap the Add Contacts button, which features a plus sign (+), to open the Contacts app, and tap on a name there to add that person as an addressee.

3. **If you want to send a copy of the e-mail to somebody, tap the Options button to make the Cc and Bcc fields appear; then, enter addresses or choose them from the Contacts app by tapping the Add Contacts button.**

4. **Tap in the Subject field and enter a subject by using the onscreen keyboard.**

5. **Tap in the Message text field and enter a message.**

6. **(Optional) If you want to add an attachment to an e-mail, tap the Options link shown near the top of the screen and press the Attach button. In the menu that appears, choose to attach an item from OfficeSuite, Personal Videos, or Photos.**

7. **To send your message, tap the Send button at the top right corner of the screen.**

If you decide you're not ready to send the message quite yet, you can press the Cancel button. A pop-up appears with options to Save Draft or Delete Draft.

Here are a couple of handy shortcuts for entering text in your e-mail: The Auto Complete feature lists possible word matches as you type; tap one to complete a word. In addition, you can double-tap the space bar to place a period and space at the end of a sentence.

Receiving e-mail

Kindle Fire HD can receive your e-mail messages whenever you're connected to a Wireless network.

When an e-mail is delivered to your inbox (see Figure 5-10), simply tap to open it. Read it, and contemplate whether you want to save it or delete it (or forward or reply to it, as covered in the following section). If you don't need to keep the message, you can delete it by tapping the Delete button in the Options bar.

Forwarding and replying to e-mail

When you receive an e-mail, you can choose to reply to the sender, reply to the sender and anybody else who was included as an addressee on the original message, or forward the e-mail to another person.

If you reply to all recipients, you send an answer to the sender, anybody else in the To: field of the original message, and anybody in the Cc: and Bcc: fields. Because Bcc: fields aren't visible to you as a recipient, you may be sending your reply to people you're not aware of.

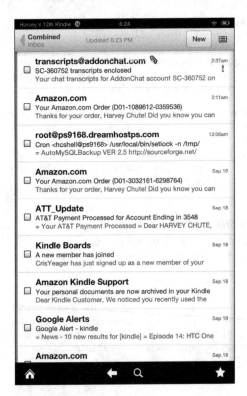

Figure 5-10: Your inbox.

To forward or reply to an e-mail, with the Email app inbox displayed, follow these steps:

1. **Tap an e-mail to open it.**

2. **Tap the Respond button.**

   A menu of options appears.

3. **Tap Reply, Reply All, or Forward.**

4. **If you're forwarding the message, enter a new recipient.**

   If you're replying, the message is already addressed, but you can enter additional recipients if you want to.

5. **Tap in the message area and enter your message.**

6. **Tap the Send button to send your message on its way.**

Sending E-Mail to Your Kindle Account

When you register your Kindle Fire HD, you get an associated e-mail account.

The address of the account is displayed in the Docs library. Tap the Docs Library button on the Home screen, and you see a line that reads Send Documents to *YourE-MailAccount*@kindle.com where *Your E-Mail Account* is the name of your Kindle e-mail account.

You or others can e-mail documents to this address, and those documents automatically appear in your Docs library. Note that you might need to go to Amazon by using a browser and change the approved e-mail accounts. Click on Your Account and then on Manage Your Kindle. Click the Personal Document Settings, and make sure the account is listed under Send to Kindle Email Settings as approved.

Chapter 6

Books, Videos, and Music

● ●

In This Chapter

▶ Finding what's available to read

▶ Flipping through periodicals

▶ Streaming or downloading videos

▶ Watching movies and TV shows

▶ Checking out the Music library

▶ Getting music onto the Cloud

● ●

*T*his chapter is all about consuming content. Here, you discover what's available to read, how to open publications, and how to read and then delete them from Kindle Fire HD when you're finished. After talking about the Kindle e-reader, I explain how Amazon streams video content from the Cloud to your device. Then, I give you a look at the Kindle Fire HD Video library and cover the steps involved in playing a video. Finally, I show you how to get music onto your Kindle Fire HD (see Chapter 4 for more about shopping for music) and how to use the simple tools in the library to play your music and create playlists.

E-Reader Extraordinaire

Kindle Fire HD comes from a family of e-readers, so
it's only natural that the e-reader you use to read
books and magazines on the device is a very robust
feature. With its bright, colorful screen, Kindle Fire
HD broadens your reading experience beyond black
and white books to color publications such as
magazines or graphic novels. The Kindle Fire HD's
easy-to-use controls help you navigate publications,
bookmark and highlight text, and search your libraries
of print content.

So Many Things to Read

Amazon started as an online book retailer, although
through the years, it has branched out to become the
largest retailer of just about everything on the planet.
Kindle Fire HD makes it easy for you to buy your
content from Amazon. Although you can buy and
sideload content from other sources to Kindle Fire HD,
buying from Amazon ensures that you're dealing with
a reputable company and receiving safe content
(uncontaminated by malware).

The content you buy from Amazon is automatically
downloaded to your Kindle device, which means that
not only is buying from Amazon's bookstore easy, but
you can take advantage of its vast selection of books.
In addition, you can borrow Kindle versions of books
from many public libraries.

Amazon has also made deals to make many of your
favorite magazines and newspapers available. With
magazines and newspapers, you can buy the current
issue or subscribe to get multiple issues sent to your
Kindle Fire HD as they become available.

To buy books or magazines for your Kindle Fire HD, on the Home screen, tap either the Books or Newsstand button, which takes you to your Books or Magazine library.

Tap the Store button; this takes you to the Amazon Kindle bookstore, shown in Figure 6-1. (See Chapter 4 for more about how to search for and buy content.)

Figure 6-1: Buy magazines by the issue or subscribe by using Newsstand.

You can also buy content at the Amazon website from your computer and have it download to your Kindle Fire HD. Just select what device you want it delivered to from the drop-down list below the Add to Cart button before you buy Kindle content.

Reading Books

After you own some Kindle books, you can begin to read by using the simple e-reader tools in the Kindle e-reader app. You may have used this app on another device, such as your computer, smartphone, or tablet, although each version of this app has slightly different features. In the following sections, I go over the basics of how the Kindle e-reader app works on Kindle Fire HD.

 You can get to the Home screen from anywhere in the e-reader app. If a Home button isn't visible, just tap the bottom of the page to display the Options bar which includes a Home button.

Going to the (Books) library

When you tap Books on your Kindle Fire HD Home screen, you open the Books library, containing downloaded content on the Device tab and content in the Cloud on the Cloud tab (see Figure 6-2). The active tab is the one displaying orange text. There's also a Store link you use to go to Amazon's website and shop for books.

There are several features in your Books library that you can use to get different perspectives on its contents:

> ✔ **Grid and List views.** Tap Menu on the Options
>   bar to display the Grid View and List View
>   options. These provide views of your books by
>   using large thumbnails on a bookshelf or in a
>   text list including title and author, along with an
>   accompanying small thumbnail.

Figure 6-2: The Books library displays all your book purchases
on two tabs.

✔ **Sort titles.** Use the By Author, By Recent, and By Title buttons to view books by any of these three criteria.

✔ **Identify new titles.** If you've just downloaded but haven't started reading a book, there will be a grey banner in the corner of the thumbnail with the word New in it (see Figure 6-3).

Tap the Search button on the Options bar to search your Books library contents by title or author.

Figure 6-3: New titles are easily identifiable.

Opening a book

To open a book from the Home screen, tap Books to open the Books library. Locate the book you want to read (swipe upward if you need to reveal more books in the list), and simply tap it. If the book has not been downloaded to your Kindle Fire HD, it begins to download and takes only seconds to complete.

If you've never begun to read the book, it opens on its title page. If you've read part of the book, it opens automatically to the last page you read. This last read page is bookmarked in the Cloud by Amazon when you stop reading, so no matter what device you use to read it — your Kindle Fire HD, computer, or smartphone, for example — you go to the last read page immediately.

You can also open a publication from Favorites or the Carousel. Read more about these features in Chapter 2.

Navigating a book

The simplest way to move one page forward or one page back is to tap your finger anywhere on the right or left side of the page, respectively. Try this to move from the title page to a page of text within the book. With a book page displayed, tap it near the center of the page to see the tools shown in Figure 6-4, including a button to take you to the Kindle Fire HD Home screen, a Back button to go back to the previous screen, a Search button to initiate a search for text in the book, and the Favorites "star" icon to bring up your favorite items.

Figure 6-4: Navigation tools in Kindle e-reader.

At the top of the screen is a list of useful functions: Settings, Go To, Notes, X-Ray, Share, and Bookmark. We will look at each of those in turn in the following sections.

Settings: Modifying how a page looks

There are several things you can do to control how things appear on a page in Kindle e-reader. First, you can make text larger or smaller. You can choose a white, black, or sepia-toned background for a page. And finally, you can change the font type.

To control all these settings, tap the page to display the Options bar, and then tap the Settings button (the one with a capital and lowercase A). The options shown in Figure 6-5 appear:

- **Font Size:** Tap the large or the small font button to progressively increase or decrease the font size.

- **Color Mode (black on white, black on sepia, white on black):** Tap a setting to display a different color page background. A sepia background may make reading easier on your eyes, for example.

- **Margins:** Tap a setting to change the margin width to Narrow, Normal, or Wide.

- **Font:** Change the font to one of five different font types.

- **Text-to-Speech:** Turn on or off the automatic reading of the book by Kindle's Text-to-Speech function.

Go to: Jumping to different parts of a book

You can also tap the Go To button in the Options bar and choose from these options to move around your book:

- **Go to Page or Location:** A pop-up will appear asking for a Page or Location, as shown in figure 6-6. Enter the desired Page or Location, and press the appropriate button (Page or Location). Location is calculated by the number of bits of information in the book up to the current location. You can note the location of a particular page by checking this information above the progress bar at the bottom of any page.

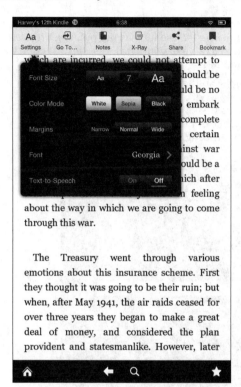

which are incurred, we could not attempt to ... hould be ... ld be no ... embark ... complete ... certain ... inst war ... uld be a ... ich after ... feeling about the way in which we are going to come through this war.

The Treasury went through various emotions about this insurance scheme. First they thought it was going to be their ruin; but when, after May 1941, the air raids ceased for over three years they began to make a great deal of money, and considered the plan provident and statesmanlike. However, later

Figure 6-5: Font options offer you some control over the appearance of your pages.

- ✔ **Sync to Furthest Page:** This option moves you to the last page you read in the book with any Kindle reader apps or devices.
- ✔ **Beginning:** This option allows you to return to the beginning of the book.
- ✔ **Cover:** Choosing this option will take you to the book's cover.

✔ **Table of Contents:** Each item in the table of contents is listed (so long as the publisher has provided a table of contents). Just tap a section to jump to it.

✔ **End:** Tap the End link to go to the end of the book, where the Before You Go page is displayed. This page allows you to review and rate the book and share your thoughts about the book through social media.

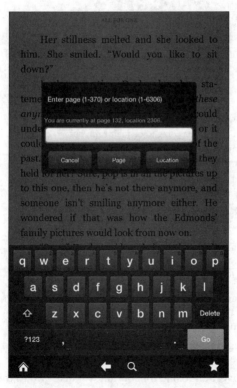

Figure 6-6: Enter a location in the book to jump there instantly.

Notes: Show your notes, highlights, and bookmarks

Tap the Notes link to view any notes, highlights, and bookmarks that you have inserted in the book (see more about how to do this in the sections "Bookmark: Save your place in a book" and "Highlighting," later in this chapter), as shown in Figure 6-7. Tap a selection to go that page.

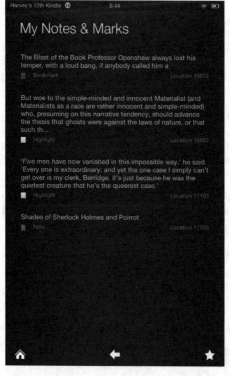

Figure 6-7: A list of your bookmarks, highlights, and notes.

X-Ray: Look into the "bones" of your book

Tap the X-Ray option to look at summary information about the book. Some e-books – more and more — have the X-Ray feature enabled. This feature provides a view into the recurring items of the e-book: characters, settings, topics, and phrases that occur throughout the book.

You can view this information for the current page, the current chapter, or the entire e-book. Tap on any term to bring up additional information from Wikipedia and from Shelfari, a community-driven website for collecting and sharing book information.

Share: Share your thoughts about the book with the Kindle community

Tap the Share button to view the Shared Notes & Highlights page. This page allows you to post a note about the book and share it through Twitter and/or Facebook.

The page also shows other people's notes and highlights that they have recently shared from this book.

Bookmark: Save your place in a book

If you find that perfect quote or a section you just have to read again at a later time, you can use the Bookmark feature in Kindle e-reader.

To place a bookmark on a page, display the page. Tap the page to reveal the Bookmark button in the top-right corner, and then tap the button. A small bookmark ribbon appears on the page (see Figure 6-8).

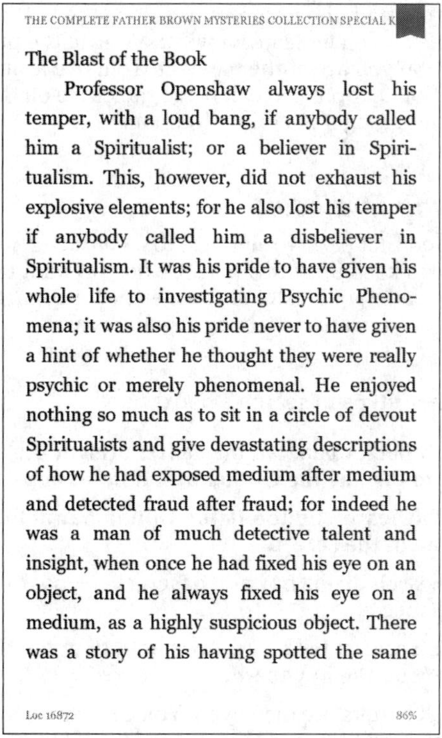

THE COMPLETE FATHER BROWN MYSTERIES COLLECTION SPECIAL K

The Blast of the Book

Professor Openshaw always lost his temper, with a loud bang, if anybody called him a Spiritualist; or a believer in Spiritualism. This, however, did not exhaust his explosive elements; for he also lost his temper if anybody called him a disbeliever in Spiritualism. It was his pride to have given his whole life to investigating Psychic Phenomena; it was also his pride never to have given a hint of whether he thought they were really psychic or merely phenomenal. He enjoyed nothing so much as to sit in a circle of devout Spiritualists and give devastating descriptions of how he had exposed medium after medium and detected fraud after fraud; for indeed he was a man of much detective talent and insight, when once he had fixed his eye on an object, and he always fixed his eye on a medium, as a highly suspicious object. There was a story of his having spotted the same

Loc 16872   86%

Figure 6-8: A bookmarked page.

This gives you an easy way to get back to the current page later. You can bookmark multiple pages in the book if there are several sections that you want to easily view later.

As you read, the progress bar along the bottom of the screen indicates how far along in the publication you are at the moment. To move around the publication, you can press the circle on this bar and drag it in either direction.

Searching in a book

Want to find that earlier reference to a character so that you can keep up with a plot? Or do you want to find any mention of Einstein in an e-encyclopedia? To find words or phrases in a book, use the Search feature.

Follow these steps to search a book:

1. **With a book open, tap the center area of the page to display the Option bar, if necessary.**

2. **Tap the Search button in the Option bar at the bottom of the screen.**

   The Search dialog box and onscreen keyboard are displayed.

3. **Enter a search term or phrase, and then tap the Go key on the keyboard.**

   Search results are displayed. You can tap on a search result to go to that page of the book.

Highlighting

To highlight text, press and hold your finger at the beginning of the text, and drag your finger to the end of the text. The selected text is highlighted in blue, as shown in Figure 6-9.

Small grey handles appear on either side of the selected text. If you want to select additional adjacent text to be highlighted, press your finger on one of these handles and drag to the left or right.

A set of buttons appear above the selected text. Press Note to add a note, press Highlight to highlight the text, or press Share to post the selected text to social media.

There is also a More button, which brings up a set of options to Search for the selected text in the Book, on Wikipedia, or on the web.

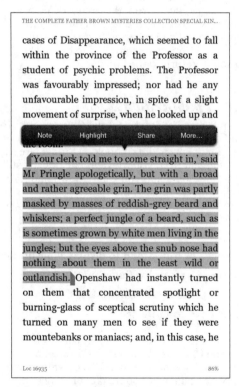

THE COMPLETE FATHER BROWN MYSTERIES COLLECTION SPECIAL KIN...

cases of Disappearance, which seemed to fall within the province of the Professor as a student of psychic problems. The Professor was favourably impressed; nor had he any unfavourable impression, in spite of a slight movement of surprise, when he looked up and

| Note | Highlight | Share | More... |

'Your clerk told me to come straight in,' said Mr Pringle apologetically, but with a broad and rather agreeable grin. The grin was partly masked by masses of reddish-grey beard and whiskers; a perfect jungle of a beard, such as is sometimes grown by white men living in the jungles; but the eyes above the snub nose had nothing about them in the least wild or outlandish. Openshaw had instantly turned on them that concentrated spotlight or burning-glass of sceptical scrutiny which he turned on many men to see if they were mountebanks or maniacs; and, in this case, he

Loc 16935   86%

Figure 6-9: Click either handle to enlarge the area of selected text.

When you place a bookmark on a page or highlight text within a book, you can then display a list of bookmarks and highlights by tapping the Notes button in the Option bar. You can jump to the page indicated by a bookmark or to highlighted text by tapping an item in this list.

 When you press and hold on a word in the book, you see the pop-up shown in Figure 6-10, a brief definition appears from the pre-installed New Oxford American Dictionary. In the definition window, tap Full Definition to go to the full Oxford dictionary definition. Tap the Back button to return to the book.

Managing publications

After you purchase content on Amazon, from apps to music and books, it's archived in your Amazon Cloud library. If you finish reading a book on Kindle Fire HD, you can remove it from your device. The book is still in the Amazon Cloud, and you can re-download it to your Kindle Fire HD at any time.

To remove a book or magazine from your Book library, follow these steps:

1. **Tap Books or Newsstand to display your library.**

2. **Locate and press your finger on the item.**

   A menu appears (see Figure 6-11).

3. **Tap Remove from Device.**

The thumbnail of the item remains in your Books library on the Cloud tab and on the Carousel or Favorites if you've placed it there. To download and read the book again, just double-tap it in any of these locations, and the download begins.

THE COMPLETE FATHER BROWN MYSTERIES COLLECTION SPECIAL KIN...

cases of Disappearance, which seemed to fall within the province of the Professor as a student of psychic problems. The Professor was favourably impressed; nor had he any unfavourable impression, in spite of a slight movement of surprise, when he looked up and saw that the Rev. Luke Pringle was already in the room.

'Your clerk told me to come straight in,' said Mr Pringle apologetically, but with a broad and rather agreeable grin. The grin was partly masked by masses of reddish-grey beard and whiskers; a perfect jungle of a beard, such as

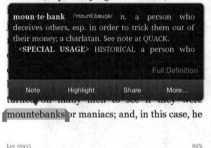

moun·te·bank /ˈmountiˌbaNGk/ *n.* a person who deceives others, esp. in order to trick them out of their money; a charlatan. See note at QUACK.
<SPECIAL USAGE> HISTORICAL a person who

Full Definition

| Note | Highlight | Share | More... |

turned on many men to see if they were mountebanks or maniacs; and, in this case, he

Loc 16935   86%

Figure 6-10: Tap and hold a word to view a dictionary definition of the word.

Unlike video and music, which you can stream from the Cloud without ever downloading them, books, magazines, and newspapers can't be read from the Cloud. They must be downloaded to a Kindle device before you can read them.

Figure 6-11: Use this menu to remove a publication from Kindle Fire HD.

Reading Periodicals

Reading magazines and newspapers on your Kindle Fire HD is similar to reading books, with a few important differences. You navigate magazines a bit differently and can display them in two different views.

Follow these steps to read a magazine or newspaper:

1. **From the Home screen, tap Newsstand.**

2. **Tap a magazine or newspaper in the Newsstand to read it.**

   Alternatively, you can tap an item on the Carousel from the Home screen.

   If the publication hasn't been downloaded to the device, it begins to download now.

   With the Options bar visible, thumbnails of all pages in the publication are displayed along the bottom of the screen (see Figure 6-12).

3. **Swipe right or left to scroll through these pages.**

4. **When you find the page you want, tap that page to display it full screen.**

   The Menu button on the Options bar displays contents of the current issue.

5. **Tap the Table of Contents icon in the lower part of the screen, and tap an item in the table of contents to go to that item.**

 As with books, you can double-tap to enlarge text on the page; double-tap again to reduce the size of the text. You can also pinch and unpinch the touchscreen to move between larger and smaller views of a page's contents.

Some periodicals can appear in two views:

✔ **Text view:** In Text view, you see articles in more of an e-reader format (meaning that you get larger text with no columns and no images). In Text view, there's a Font button on the Options bar offering Font Style and Typeface tabs to adjust the size and font used for text. There's also a Style choice for changing Size, Spacing, Margins, and Color Mode (page background).

✔ **Page view:** Page view shows an exact image of the publication's pages, with all columns and photos intact. You can scroll through the magazine, view it in landscape or portrait orientation, and pinch and unpinch to zoom in and out of the pages.

If Text View is available for a magazine, you can double-tap the article to switch between Page View and Text View.

Figure 6-12: Scroll through thumbnails of pages to find the one you want.

Playing Videos

Playing video, both movies and TV shows, is a great use of Kindle Fire HD. The device has a bright, high-definition screen, can easily be held in one hand, and is capable of streaming video from the Cloud, making a typically seamless viewing experience without hogging memory on the tablet itself.

In addition, Amazon offers an amazing selection of video content, including absolutely free Prime Instant Videos (as long as you maintain a Prime account with Amazon).

Streaming versus downloading

When you tap the Video button on the Kindle Fire HD Home screen, you're immediately taken to the Amazon Video Store (see Figure 6-13), rather than to a library of video titles. That makes sense because, by design, Kindle Fire HD is best used to stream videos from the Cloud. Even with the device's considerable memory (16GB or 32GB – and up to 64GB for the Kindle Fire HD 4G LTE model), it can't accommodate a large number of HD video files; instead, Amazon makes it easy for you to stream video to the device without ever downloading it. To go to your Video library, tap the Library button in the top-right corner.

Video content might include Prime Instant Videos, a feature which offers thousands of titles for free with an Amazon Prime account. (You get one free month of Amazon Prime with your Kindle Fire HD, after which you can purchase a membership for $79 a year.) You can also purchase or rent other video programs and stream them from the Cloud.

Figure 6-13: The Amazon Video Store offers thousands of titles.

Amazon's Whispersync technology keeps track of the spot in a video where you stopped watching. You can later resume watching that video at that exact location on Kindle Fire HD, a PC or Mac, or one of over 300 compatible TVs, Blu-ray Disc players, or other devices.

You *can* download videos you purchase (you can't download Prime Instant Videos, however), which is useful if you want to watch them away from a Wi-Fi connection. It's a good idea to remove them from the device when you're done to save space. To delete a video from your device, open the Video library, and tap the Device tab. Press and hold your finger on the video, and then tap Remove from Device in the menu that appears.

Looking at your video library

The Kindle Fire HD Video library may become your favorite destination for buying, viewing, and organizing your video content.

When you tap Video on your Kindle Fire HD Home screen, the Amazon Video Store opens.

The Store shows a featured video and various video categories, such as Prime Instant Videos, Next Up, Movies, and TV Shows. Scroll through the available movies by swiping to the right or left. Or, tap the See More link to see a screen full of available videos.

Tap the Library button to go to your Video library (see Figure 6-14). The library sports two tabs — one lists all your videos stored in the Cloud, and one includes videos you've purchased that have been downloaded to the device. The tab that has orange lettering is the active tab.

In addition to the Cloud and Device tabs, there are tabs for filtering content by Movies or TV programs. Note that there's no search function you can use to find the content you're looking for.

Figure 6-14: The Kindle Fire HD Video library.

 Downloaded video content is listed chronologically by the date you downloaded it.

Tap the Menu button on the Options bar to display four items — Settings, Your Watchlist, Sort By, and Help & Feedback.

In Settings (see Figure 6-15), you can change your download settings to specify the type and quality of downloads and view the Device ID and Version number.

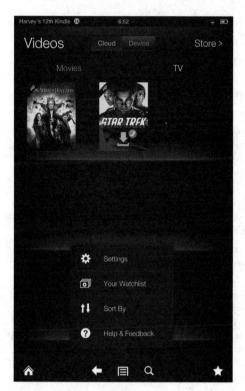

Figure 6-15: The Video Settings screen allows you to specify video download options.

Opening and playing a video

Playing a video is a simple process. If the video has been downloaded to your device, open the library (tap Video, and then tap the Library button), locate the video (using methods described in the preceding section), and then tap the video to play it.

If you're streaming a video you've purchased from the Cloud, follow these steps:

1. **Tap the Cloud tab.**

   Videos you've rented (whose rental period hasn't expired) or purchased are displayed.

2. **Tap an item to open it.**

   If it's a TV show, you see episodes listed (see Figure 6-16); tap one to open it. If it's a movie, at this point, you see a description of the movie.

3. **Tap the Watch Now button.**

   The playback controls appear.

4. **If you've already watched part of the video, tap the Resume button.**

   If you'd rather see the video from its start, tap the Start Over button.

   The movie appears full screen (see Figure 6-17). The title of the Movie appears at the top of the screen.

Note that the Kindle Fire HD screen provides an extra-wide viewing angle. This means that you and those watching with you can see the content from the side as well as from straight on.

The familiar playback tools available here include

- ✔ Play
- ✔ Pause
- ✔ A progress bar
- ✔ A volume slider
- ✔ A button that moves you ten seconds back in the video

Figure 6-16: The episode list for a TV show.

Also, if the video is enabled for X-Ray, you can tap the screen to see a list and photos of cast members. Tap on a cast member to see more info. This is a unique feature offered by Amazon in collaboration with its IMDB (Internet Movie Database) group.

There's also a Back button in the Options bar on the right side of the display that you can tap to stop playback and return to the Kindle Fire HD Video library.

The More Episodes button goes back to all episodes of a TV show.

Figure 6-17: A movie with playback controls on Kindle Fire HD.

When you display a video's details in the Amazon Video Store, you can tap the Rental & Purchase Details link to view the terms of use for playing the video.

Playing Music

The ability to tap into Amazon's tremendous Music Store and sideload music from other sources by using a Micro USB cable means that you can build up your ideal Music library and take it with you wherever you go.

Exploring the Music library

All your music is stored in the Music library (see Figure 6-18), which you display by tapping the Music button on the Kindle Fire HD Home screen.

The library is organized by Playlists, Artists, Albums, and Songs. Tap on any of these tabs to display the associated content.

Figure 6-18: The Music library is your central music repository.

At the bottom of the screen, in the Options bar, is a Back arrow to move you back one screen in the library, the Menu icon, and a Search icon to help you find pieces of music.

If you tap the Menu button, you see these additional options:

- ✔ **List View / Grid View:** This menu option toggles to let you switch from the default Grid View to a simpler List View of your music content.

- ✔ **Downloads:** Tap Downloads to see items in the process of downloading, as well as completed downloads.

- ✔ **Settings:** Tap Settings to see options for entering an Amazon claim code, clearing the cache, enabling equalizer mode, and more.

- ✔ **Clear Player:** Tap the Clear Queue command to stop the music and go back to the Music library home screen.

- ✔ **Help:** Tap Help to get more information about using the Music app.

 When you tap the Search button on the Options bar, you bring up a search field. Tap in the field and enter the title of a piece of music or a performer, and then tap Go on the onscreen keyboard. Kindle Fire HD displays results on each of the tabs in the Music library (Artist, Album, and Song) that match the search term(s).

Uploading music to the Cloud

One way to add music to your Kindle Fire HD Music library is by buying it from the Amazon Music Store.

You can also transfer a musical selection or collection stored on your computer (the music you've bought through iTunes, for example) by using a Micro USB cable connection. (Read more about this process in Chapter 2.)

In addition, the Amazon Cloud allows you to upload music from your computer; after you upload music, it's available to you through your Kindle Fire HD Music library.

Follow these steps to upload music to the Amazon Cloud:

1. **Go to** www.amazon.com/cloudplayer **on your PC or Mac.**

2. **Sign into your Amazon account.**

3. **Tap the Import Your Music button.**

   A dialog box appears, asking you to get the Amazon MP3 Importer.

4. **Tap Download Now, and follow the instructions that appear to install the Importer.**

   After the Importer has been installed, you see the Import dialog box shown in Figure 6-19.

5. **Follow the Scan, Select, and Import steps to import some or all of your music to the Amazon Cloud.**

Figure 6-19: Tap into all your music by using the Importer.

After you upload items to your Amazon Cloud library, they are available to Kindle Fire HD on the Cloud tab of the Music library.

Opening and playing a song

After you have some music available to play (which I discussed in the preceding sections), playing that music is an easy task.

First, you locate an item to play, and then you can use the playback toolbar to control the playback. Follow these steps to play music from your Music library:

1. **Tap the Music button on the Kindle Fire HD Home screen.**

2. **Locate an item you want to play on a tab in the Music library, such as Songs or Artists.**

3. **If you open a tab other than Songs, you need to tap to open an album or playlist to view the contents.**

4. **Tap to play it.**

   If you tap the first song in a group of music selections, such as an album or playlist, Kindle Fire HD begins to play all selections, starting with the one you tapped.

5. **Use the controls shown in Figure 6-20 to control playback.**

Tap the Back button to go back to the album or playlist the song belongs to. To go back to the Now Playing screen for the song, tap the lower part of the screen that displays the current song (see Figure 6-21).

You can adjust playback volume by tapping Quick Settings and then Volume, or use the Volume setting in the Now Playing controls.

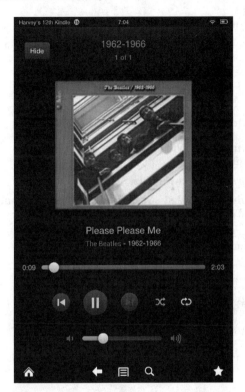

Figure 6-20: Most of these tools are standard playback tools you've probably seen before.

Figure 6-21: The currently playing song sports a little orange speaker in this list.

Creating playlists

When you tap Music on the Home screen, you see the Playlists tab. Tap it, and you see your playlists along with two default playlists, Purchases and Recently Added to Cloud. There's also a Create New Playlist button.

To create a new playlist, follow these steps:

1. **Connect to a Wi-Fi network if you aren't already connected.**

2. **Tap Create New Playlist.**

3. **In the screen that appears, enter a playlist name and tap Save.**

4. **Tap the Add Song (+) button to the right of any song to select it.**

   To find a song without scrolling down the list, enter a song name in the Search field.

5. **Tap Done to save your playlist.**

   The Playlist is displayed and includes an Edit button that you can tap to edit the playlist.

To play newly created playlist, simply tap the Playlist tab and then the list you want to play.

 When you tap the Edit button on a playlist, you see an Add button and a Done button in the Edit screen. Songs appear with a Delete (–) symbol next to them; tap this symbol to delete a song. Tap Add (+) to choose more songs to add to the playlist. Tap Done when you're done editing.

Chapter 7

Ten Apps That Add Functionality

● ●

In This Chapter

▶ Writing and drawing with your Kindle Fire HD

▶ Going by the numbers

▶ Keeping your schedule organized

▶ Monitoring your connection

● ●

Kindle Fire HD has functionality built in for consuming books, periodicals, music, and video, as well as a contact management app, web browser, and e-mail client. And, by adding apps to the device, you can easily acquire those tools you use regularly but that don't happen to be built into the Kindle Fire HD.

The Amazon Appstore, which you can learn to use in Chapter 4, contains thousands of cool apps for you to explore. To help you flesh out the basic tools in Kindle Fire HD, in this chapter, I provide reviews of apps such as a calendar, note taker, and unit converter that meet your day-to-day needs and whet your appetite. Most of these are free.

From a nutrition guide to a very cool calculator app, these will provide fun and functionality for your Kindle Fire HD and not cost you much more than the time to download them.

SketchBook Mobile Express

From: AutoDesk, Inc.

Price: Free

SketchBook is a drawing app to satisfy the creative artist in your soul. With 47 preset brushes, you can draw whatever you can imagine on your Kindle Fire HD screen. You can control the brush characteristics and make use of an extensive color palette.

Try sideloading photos and modifying them with this clever app, and then save your files in JPEG, PNG, or PSD formats. When you're done, it's easy to e-mail your artistic efforts to yourself to print from your computer.

The Brush Properties circular control lets you easily adjust the size and opacity of the writing tools. Touch the square at the top of the screen to access color controls and watch the Red, Blue, and Green levels adjust as you move around the color wheel.

Fast Food Nutrition Lite

From: FastFood.com

Price: Free

If you're watching your weight but are forced to scarf down fast food now and then, this little app could have an impact on your waistline. Not limited to traditional drive-thru fast food joints, the app gives you nutritional information about dishes from 100 restaurant chains, such as Applebee's, Chili's, and Checker's, and it includes over 25,000 menu items.

Fast Food Nutrition Lite helps you keep track of calories, Weight Watchers points, fats, trans fats, saturated fats, cholesterol, sodium, carbohydrates, sugars, and protein. The calorie counter shows you how much of the recommended daily allowance each meal is providing you. Select the items you want in your meal and touch View Order, which displays a handy screen showing you all the totals for your meal.

You can add thumbnails for your favorite restaurants so that you don't have to search through all the restaurants to find the ones you like best.

aCalendar

From: Mathias Laabs

Price: Free

Kindle Fire HD has no built-in calendar app, so this one is a natural to add to your apps collection. This easy-to-use calendar app can help keep you on schedule. You can display day, week, month, and birthday views. For you astronomers out there, you can even check the phases of the moon. The month screen displays black dots for full moons and a half-filled dot to indicate a half moon.

aCalendar makes great use of touchscreen gestures to let you easily move among views and take a look at event details. Swipe the screen horizontally to change among day, week, and month views. Swipe vertically to move from day to day, week to week, or month to month.

You can also add events to your calendar by simply pressing a date and filling in the name and time of your event.

Astral Budget

From: Astral Web, Inc.

Price: Free

Astral Budget helps you keep track of all your expenses, whether for a single trip or your yearly household budget. You can use built-in categories for fixed spending such as rent, food, travel, utilities, and so on to categorize your expenses.

The app has four sections: Goals, Expenses, Reports, and Export. Using these, you can enter the amounts you want to spend and track them against actual expenditures. You can use the wide variety of Reports in Astral Budget to examine your spending trends and even export data to your computer to examine with the more-robust application Excel. I like the Chart selections, including bar charts, pie charts, and list charts.

ColorNote Notepad Notes

From: Social & Mobile, Inc.

Price: Free

If being able to keep a to-do list warms the cockles of your organized (or disorganized) heart, this note-taking app is free and very simple to use.

You can keep a simple to-do list or other random notes and even share information with your friends via e-mail, social networks, or messaging.

ColorNote allows some nice word-processing-like functions, such as the capability to edit and cross items off lists that are completed.

You can even set up reminders for items in your notes and search for specific content.

 If your notes are top secret, consider using the password feature in ColorNote.

Cube Calculator

From: IP

Price: Free

This is a calculator with tons of bells and whistles, from the ability to use mathematical expressions and time calculations to logarithmic and trigonometric functions. There's a secondary keyboard for additional functions, such as cosines.

Even if you're not a power math user, the very nice interface in this app makes casual calculations simple to do. Also, the help system for this app is actually helpful.

You can choose a theme such as Light or Dark to ease your eyestrain as you calculate. You can also control the maximum number of digits to be returned in a result.

Handrite Note

From: Ben Lee

Price: $2.99

If you miss the feeling of writing notes by hand, instead of typing them on plastic keyboards, this app is for you. It's simple to use: Tap to create a new note, and then use the spiral-bound pad interface to write words or draw images on the page with your finger. You can change the stroke width and text size for your writing and even use different colors.

When you close the app, your note is saved, but you can press and hold the touchscreen to edit the text you entered. You can also create a label for a note and export it. The app isn't fancy; it's more for jotting down a phone number when you see a flyer about a missing kitten or making a quick note to yourself about what to pick up at the store. But for what it is, it's handy and easy to use.

Exchange by TouchDown

From: NitroDesk, Inc.

Price: Free

If you want to access e-mail, contacts, and calendar information from your workplace, and your company uses Microsoft Exchange Server for these accounts, this little app will help you tap into your company e-mail. It touts itself as providing great security and provides the very handy service of wiping data from your Kindle Fire HD remotely if it's lost or stolen.

Keep in mind that TouchDown doesn't work with IMAP or POP3 servers; it's intended for Exchange Servers, as well as supporting Zimbra, Kerio, and ActiveSync. Although the app has pretty-easy-to-use settings, you might want to sit down over a cup of coffee with your network administrator to get this one working.

Units

From: staticfree.info

Price: Free

If, like me, you need help converting just about anything to anything else (feet to meters, pounds to kilos, or whatever), you'll appreciate this handy little app. It handles 2,400 different conversions, including height, weight, volume, volume to weight, and time to distance. Tap the Unit key, and you'll see a list of the various types of conversions available.

Just fill in the You Have field and the You Want field, and then enter the number of units. Tap the equal sign (=) and get your conversion. Holding Kindle Fire HD in landscape orientation displays a few more helpful tools on the calculator style interface.

Wi-Fi Analyzer

From: farproc

Price: Free

Because most Kindle Fire HD models can connect to the web only through Wi-Fi, this handy app is helpful for keeping track of local Wi-Fi connections. You can observe available Wi-Fi channels and the signal strength on each. There are several styles of graphs to choose from, including Channel, Time, Channel Rating, and Signal Meter.